Odd Man Out

INDIANA UNIVERSITY PRESS FILMGUIDE SERIES
Harry M. Geduld and Ronald Gottesman,
General Editors

Filmguide to

Odd Man Out

JAMES DeFELICE

INDIANA UNIVERSITY PRESS
Bloomington   London

Published in Canada by Fitzhenry & Whiteside Limited, Don Mills, Ontario
Manufactured in the United States of America

cc

Library of Congress Cataloging in Publication Data
DeFelice, James.
   Filmguide to Odd man out.
   "A Carol Reed Filmography"
   Bibliography
   1. Odd man out (Motion picture) I. Title.
PN1997.026D4   1975   791.43'7   74-6519
ISBN 0-253-39317-5 cl.
ISBN 0-253-39318-3 pbk.

contents

preface

I would like to thank the staff of the Lincoln Center Library of the Performing Arts, New York for the assistance in researching this book; Wayne Gill of the University of Alberta for his technical help, and Harry Geduld and Ronald Gottesman, the editors, for their invaluable guidance and perceptive observations.

Filmguide to

Odd Man Out

credits

ODD MAN OUT

J. Arthur Rank Production, 1947, A Two Cities Film

Screenplay	F. L. Green and R. C. Sherriff
Direction	Carol Reed
Director of Photography	Robert Krasker
Production Decor	Roger Furse
Art Director	Ralph Brinton
Editor	Fergus McDonell
Music Composed by	William Alwyn
Camera Operator	Russell Thompson
Sound Recordists	A. Fisher and Desmond Dew
Sound Editor	Harry Miller
Time	116 minutes

Filmed in Belfast, Ireland, and Denham Studios.

London Premiere: January 30, 1947, Odeon Cinema, Leicester Square.
New York Premiere: April 23, 1947, Loew's Criterion.

CAST

Johnny	James Mason
Lukey	Robert Newton
Kathleen	Kathleen Ryan
Dennis	Robert Beatty
Fencie	William Hartnell
Shell	F. J. McCormick
Rosie	Fay Compton
Maudie	Beryl Measor
Pat	Cyril Cusack
Tober	Elwyn Brook-Jones
Nolan	Dan O'Herlihy
Murphy	Roy Irving
Teresa	Maureen Delany
Granny	Kitty Kirwan
Housekeeper	Min Milligan
Gin Jimmy	Joseph Tomelty
Father Tom	W. G. Fay
Tom	Arthur Hambling
Head Constable	Denis O'Dea

and

Anne Clery, Maura Milligan, Eddie Byrne, Maureen Cusack, Pat
McGrath, Dora Bryan.

outline

Odd Man Out

1. INTRODUCTION. Aerial view of city, hill, harbor. Bell tower: four o'clock. Children playing. Dennis at book shop. Little girl crying. Granny standing in doorway, nods to Dennis. Dennis enters Johnny's room, where the gang has assembled.

2. THE ROBBERY IS PLANNED. Johnny sits on bed near window. The clock chimes. Pat, Nolan, Murphy, Johnny talk about car. Johnny warns Pat about using gun. Dennis tells Johnny his heart is not in the job. Close-ups of Kathleen listening intently. Johnny speaks out against violence. Dennis, dubious about Johnny's fitness for the job and his feelings about it, offers to go in Johnny's place. Kathleen also urges Johnny not to go. As the scene ends, Johnny asks Kathleen, "Will you be here when I come back?"

3. THE ROBBERY. Close-up through windshield of car, Pat driving. "Subjective" traveling shots of buildings; Johnny is dizzy, everything out of focus. Johnny, Nolan, Murphy enter mill, hold employees at bay (mill noises). Johnny stuffs bills into briefcase. Exterior: peddler driving coal cart, almost blocks street. Burglar alarm. Johnny dazed on mill steps, clerk tries to apprehend him. Johnny and clerk fight: clerk is killed, Johnny wounded. The car starts, Johnny half out of the vehicle. Johnny falls from car, flees out of sight with a dog pursuing him. Johnny hides in air raid shelter. Police check identity cards.

4. JOHNNY IS HUNTED. Street-urchins play at being Johnny. Murphy, Nolan, and Pat blame each other for losing Johnny. Ball kicked into shelter. Shy little girl with a skate. Johnny thinks he is dreaming; the little girl "becomes" the prison guard. Dennis puts on bandages, sets out to find Johnny. Pat, Murphy, Nolan

are chased by police. Pat and Nolan go to Teresa's. Johnny
drives Molly and Lennie from shelter. Teresa betrays Pat and
Nolan; they are killed. Dennis finds Johnny. Johnny asks
Dennis "Did I kill that man?" Dennis creates distraction for
Johnny's escape. The fight on the tram; Dennis is caught.

5. THE ODD MAN OUT: JOHNNY'S WANDERINGS. Truck barely
   misses Johnny. He is knocked down. Johnny is helped by
   Maudie and Rosie. Maudie and Rosie see the gun. Tom gives
   Johnny drink and sends him out into storm. Soldier puts Johnny
   in Gin Jimmy's cab. Police search house: head constable questions Kathleen; Granny conceals gun. Granny tells Kathleen
   about her past. Gin Jimmy takes Johnny to junk yard. Shell
   sees Johnny. The docks: Kathleen arranges escape by sea for
   Johnny. Kathleen is followed by head constable. The dance
   hall: "No Jitterbugging." Kathleen visits Father Tom. Shell and
   his wounded bird. Father Tom offers Shell "faith" if he brings
   Johnny to him.

6. THE QUEST FOR JOHNNY. Characters reveal why they want
   Johnny: Father Tom wants to comfort Johnny's soul; Kathleen
   wants to keep him from the law ("Rather than that, I'd take his
   life myseii"). Snow is falling. Johnny is sitting in tub in junk
   yard. Johnny tries to use phone in booth, two girls talking.
   Johnny staggers into booth of Four Winds pub. Fencie gives
   Johnny a drink, conceals him in a private "crib." Lukey's
   studio: Shell with bird cage; Lukey won't let Shell leave; Shell
   chased by Lukey; Shell tells Lukey he knows where Johnny is;
   Lukey wants to paint a portrait of Johnny; Shell leaves; Tober
   enters and gives Lukey money for drinks. Shell at junk yard:
   Johnny is missing. Shell finds piece of Johnny's bandage. Four
   Winds pub: Shell talks to Fencie about his "missing bird;"
   Johnny sees faces in beer bubbles, hears voices. Johnny yells;
   Lukey chases Shell; general riot. Lukey agrees to get rid of
   Johnny instead of going to jail for causing the pub riot.

7. JOHNNY'S LAST HOURS. Lukey's studio: Tober shares fish and
   chips with Shell; Shell asks Tober about "faith;" Lukey enters

with Johnny; Tober bandages Johnny and Lukey paints him. Kathleen at Father Tom's. Constable and Father Tom. Kathleen and seaman; she wants seaman to wait longer for Johnny. Lukey's studio: Johnny rises dazed and weakened; He envisions pictures sailing down from walls and forming rows, Father Tom superimposed on pictures; Johnny can't hear Father Tom, Johnny quotes St. Paul on charity; Shell guides Johnny from studio. Shell and Johnny walking through snow. Johnny lies in shrubs. Boys in bedroom watch snow falling. Police flashlight falls on Shell. Shell breaks shoelace. Kathleen finds Johnny at last. Police cordon moving forward, flashlights shined ahead. Kathleen fires two shots. Police return fire. Bodies of Kathleen and Johnny on ground before fence. Father Tom escorts Shell away from the scene of death. Camera tilts up to clock tower: 12 o'clock. Ship whistle, music, chimes.

the director

In his long career, Carol Reed has directed nearly every type of film from the profound to the trivial, from light comedy to historical pageant; he has made documentary, fantasy, suspense thriller, and musical films. Moreover, his styles have been as varied as his subjects. Reed's aim has always been to serve the story rather than to experiment or to be revolutionary. Reed revealed some of his theory of directing in an interview with Ezra Goodman published in *Theatre Arts* shortly after the opening of *Odd Man Out*. He told Goodman that technique for its own sake served no purpose in a film. He felt that the director should not obtrude on the story in order to show off his prowess. He believed in the story itself, in sincerity, and in transmitting a feeling about people.[1] Throughout his career critics have praised the understated quality of Reed's work. As late in his career as 1968, Pauline Kael, in her review of *Oliver!*, praised Reed's quiet, concealed art of good craftsmanship which, she said, could be considered revolutionary.[2]

Reed, whose most recent film is *The Public Eye* (1972), began his work in film in the early 1930s as a dialogue director at Ealing Studios for Basil Dean and worked as assistant director on the early films of the popular British singer Gracie Fields. Significantly, Reed's early training was in the theatre. After two years as a musical comedy juvenile, Reed made his London stage debut at the age of eighteen. An appearance in *The Terror* (1927) by Edgar Wallace, the English writer of detective stories, led to an association with Wallace. Reed directed and acted in Wallace's melodramas for five years until Wallace's untimely death in 1932. Reed was involved in the production of such plays as *The Flying Squad* (1929); *Persons Unknown* (1929); *The Calendar* (1929); *On the Spot* (1930), and *The Smokey Cell* (1931). This period certainly exerted an influence on Reed's later suspense films. In fact, it was

Wallace's connections with British Lion pictures which gave Reed his first opportunities in film.

Between 1935 and 1941, Reed directed films at an almost mass production pace. As Denis Forman observed, Reed served his apprenticeship on the studio floor.[3] During this period, Reed made some very bad films, including *Climbing High* (1938), and *A Girl Must Live* (1939), but he directed some very interesting ones as well. His concern with the thriller form showed itself to advantage in *Talk of the Devil* (1936), based on an idea of Reed's in which a man can imitate other people's voices, and *Night Train to Munich* (1940), with a script by Sydney Gilliat and Frank Launder who had written *The Lady Vanishes* (1938) for Alfred Hitchcock. The *New York Times* critic described Reed as "a brilliant newcomer" and called *Night Train to Munich* "by all odds the swiftest and most harrowing thriller to come out of England since the Hitchcock work."[4]

The two films which helped to make Reed's reputation during this period were *Bank Holiday* (1938) and *The Stars Look Down* (1939). In *Bank Holiday* Reed treated a group of strangers on holiday at the seaside resort of Brighton. According to one critic, "superficially, here was nothing more than a collection of common-place types thrown together at Brighton on an English bank holiday, except that the sum total of their individual personal dramas and experiences, subtly interwoven without the customary artifice of the omnibus film, made a richly integrated pattern previously outside the scope of the British film."[5] If *Bank Holiday* demonstrated Reed's talent to the British public, *The Stars Look Down,* adapted from an A.J. Cronin novel, helped Reed to gain an international reputation. The film is notable for its absorption of some of the styles of naturalistic British documentaries, like Alberto Cavalcanti's *Coal Face* (1936), Paul Rotha's *The Face of Britain* (1939) and John Grierson's *Industrial Britain* (1933).

The *New York Times* critic wrote that *The Stars Look Down* was directed with brilliant restraint by Reed: "faithfully performed in even the smallest role, it has caught the slow anguish of its coal-blackened people in a splendid and overwhelming film."[6] Reed's restraint became an important tool. Andrew Sarris, discussing *The*

Stars Look Down in 1956, cited Reed's handling of three key scenes in which crucial dialogue was treated in a quiet, apparently casual way: "These three scenes indicate more than the usual British restraint; this is directorial modulation of the highest order, and the beginning of Reed's oblique treatment of human confrontations."[7] *The Stars Look Down* also contains the expression of Reed's fatalism, especially in the closing scene of the trapped miners. This sense of fatalism would be strongly evident in other Reed films, including *Odd Man Out*.

Before he was 34, Reed had directed more films than would constitute most directors' entire career, and he had perfected techniques that would raise his subsequent group of films to a high level of achievement.

Reed maintained his pace during the war years and thus consolidated his craft. His experiences in location shooting and the documentary form as well as an increasing control of his material would greatly influence his later films. Reed's major work during this period include *A Letter From Home* (1941), *The New Lot* (1943), *The Way Ahead* (1944), and *The True Glory* (1945). *A Letter From Home* was a seventeen-minute short which showed the courage of England's women during the war. *The New Lot,* a British war office training film, showed the transformation of untrained civilians into front line soldiers. Reed expanded *The New Lot* into a full length film, *The Way Ahead,* in which an officer played by David Niven and a sergeant-major played by William Hartnell convert a group of unenthusiastic civilians recruited from various walks of life into a capable, self-confident unit. The script was written by Eric Ambler and Peter Ustinov. *The Way Ahead* deals compassionately, humorously, and intelligently with what it is like to be drafted, avoiding the heroics and concentrating on the problems and the people. Reed collaborated with Garson Kanin on *The True Glory,* a joint British and American documentary of the war which reconstructed the Normandy invasion from more than 10,000,000 feet of newsreels. *The True Glory* is considered one of Reed's major accomplishments and was highly honored by critics in both England and America.

The period following the war was Reed's most creative with the successive productions of *Odd Man Out* (1947), *The Fallen Idol*

(1948), *The Third Man* (1949), *Outcast of the Islands* (1951), and *The Man Between* (1953). One theme dominated Reed's work during this period—the outcast on the run. The heroes of Reed's outcast films are attractive or sympathetic "villains." The first of these was Johnny McQueen, wounded and pursued through a rain-soaked Belfast in *Odd Man Out.* Other outcasts in these films were Harry Lime in *The Third Man,* Peter Willems in *Outcast of the Islands,* and Ivo Kern in *The Man Between.*

Another similarity of *Odd Man Out, The Third Man,* and *The Man Between* is the importance of the cities where they are set. Reed, highly praised by James Agee for his depiction of Belfast as a night city in *Odd Man Out,*[8] is equally successful in portraying a decaying Vienna in *The Third Man,* and a malevolent Berlin in *The Man Between.* The tropics of Ceylon are a comparably atmospheric background for *Outcast of the Islands.* In these settings the "outcast" heroes are involved in intrigues or are pursued for some crime against society. Peter Willems both embraces and is ruined by various forms of evil. He embezzles, he betrays friendship, he deserts his wife. Ivo Kern is an opportunist who dies between the Eastern and Western zones of Berlin. Because Johnny McQueen has killed a man, he is pursued relentlessly until the girl who loves him takes him to his death under a barrage of bullets. Harry Lime, who on the surface is almost an embodiment of evil behavior, has an attractive charm and sophistication that makes him more appealing than his naive, romantic "friend" Holly Martins who shoots him during a chase in the sewers of Vienna. Reed would not deal with such complex heroes again.

The weakest of the four "outcast" films is *The Man Between.* However, *Odd Man Out, The Third Man,* and *Outcast of the Islands* are certainly three of Reed's best films, and are three of the finest films from postwar Britain. Though it shares little with the cluster of theme-related films, Reed directed another first-rate film, *The Fallen Idol,* during this period. *The Fallen Idol,* Reed's first film after *Odd Man Out* and based on a Graham Greene story, is concerned with a boy who believes his hero, a butler, has committed a murder. After this brief period, during which Reed produced some of his best work, he turned to a more eclectic approach and his subsequent films have been uneven in quality.

Reed received a number of honors during this period including first prize at the Cannes Film Festival and an Academy Award for his direction of *The Third Man,* which also won the British Film Academy Award for the best British film of the year. The *Fallen Idol* was honored at the Venice Film Festival and the New York Film Critics named Reed the best director of the year. And he was named a Knight Bachelor in 1952: Carol Reed, the prolific film director, became Sir Carol Reed. The same year the British Film Institute presented a Carol Reed Festival—which, of course, included *Odd Man Out, The Stars Look Down,* and *Bank Holiday* —and only a few years later the National Film Theatre devoted a season to the documentary films of Reed and Humphrey Jennings.

Ironically, by this time Reed's best work was behind him. Although he has continued to be active in film direction since 1952, only an occasional glimpse of his earlier achievement can be seen in such films as *Our Man in Havana* (1960) or *Oliver!* (1968). Many of his later films have been undistinguished, including *The Agony and The Ecstasy* (1965), an overblown biography of Michelangelo; *The Running Man* (1963), a hollow attempt at his earlier pursuit melodramas; *Trapeze* (1956), a hackneyed circus love story; and his most recent film, *The Public Eye* (1972), an uninspired extension of a slight one-act play. But Reed has never abandoned his directorial integrity and the large body of his work contains a number of excellent and enduring films. As we shall see, *Odd Man Out* represents Reed's directorial powers at their strongest and best.

Craftsmanship has distinguished Reed's work, especially in his skillful working with actors and writers and his meticulous attention to detail. In his survey of British films between 1945 and 1950, Denis Forman described Reed as "first and foremost . . . a master craftsman. His thorough knowledge embraces the whole of film making, from script to screen."[9]

In Reed's philosophy of directing, the actor's contribution to the film ranks high. In fact, he once suggested in an interview that the most important element in film is the way in which the actors interpret the story. "That's the creative side of it," he added. "Fine camera-work can help enormously but the most important thing is the actors who can play the characters which have been written down."[10]

Reed works his actors strenuously, demanding long rehearsals. At the same time, his consideration and his gift for commanding respect and cooperation create an atmosphere in which actors are willing to work tirelessly for him. Michael Redgrave, a veteran of a number of Reed films, has said:

> It is perhaps from Carol Reed, with whom I made my third film and with whom I was to make two more, that I learned for the first time how intimate the relationship between actor and director can be. Reed understands the actor's temperament perhaps as well as any director alive. The theatre and acting are in his blood and he is able, with infinite pains and care, to give the actor the feeling that everything is up to him and that all the director is doing is to make sure that he is being seen to his best advantage.[11]

Reed not only accepts suggestions from his actors but also draws ideas from them. Redgrave comments: "Indeed Reed frequently did ask my opinions and I think on several occasions adopted suggestions of mine." Similarly, there is the celebrated piece of dialogue concerning Swiss cuckoo clocks contributed by Orson Welles for *The Third Man.*

Reed has said that his method of working with actors was strongly influenced by an assignment early in his career as assistant director for Jack Ruben on *Java Head* in 1935: "He [Ruben] taught me that the one thing that mattered on a set was cooperation and good feeling. I don't know whether he was a very good director or not, but he had enormous enthusiasm and infected every one else with it. I learned how much generosity mattered in making films."[12] The fact that many actors including Redgrave, Ralph Richardson, Denis O'Dea, James Mason, Emlyn Williams, Margaret Lockwood, and Trevor Howard have worked with Reed on several films may be a compliment to his direction of them. Sarris has said, "Reed is probably the world's most creative director of actors."[13]

Reed has also been remarkably successful in his dramatic use of children. In *Odd Man Out* children indifferently parody the violence of the main action. A girl with one skate silently leads Dennis to Johnny McQueen's hiding place, and two boys watch the snow falling from their bedroom window as Johnny lies dying behind a shrub. In *Outcast of the Islands,* the walks between the huts of the river village are filled with children. Peter Willems is followed everywhere by a native boy who gradually assumes an unearthly quality. Reed gains a strange tension in *The Man Between* by having a boy bicycle through a bombed-out, rubble-strewn Berlin. In *The Third Man,* a crowd is led in pursuit of Holly Martins by a boy, who is both handsome and monstrous. In the same film there is the murdered caretaker's child.

In three of Reed's films, *The Fallen Idol, A Kid For Two Farthings* (1955), and *Oliver!,* a child is the focal point of the action. Reed's painstaking direction of the nine-year-old Bobby Henrey in *The Fallen Idol* won much praise and a number of awards including that of the New York Film Critics as the Best Director of the Year. (The young actor's mother wrote a book detailing the making of the film.)

A Kid For Two Farthings, based on a novel by Wolf Mankowitz, is the story of a boy who thinks a one-horned baby goat is a unicorn, and *Oliver!,* a musical based on Lionel Bart's stage version of Charles Dickens' novel, further revealed Reed's talent in directing children. *Oliver!* won an Academy Award as the Best Film of 1968 and Reed was named Best Director.

Reed believes that it is the director's responsibility to carry out the intentions of the author, and he places as strong an emphasis on working with the writer in developing the script as he does on working with the actors in realizing it. He likes to spend three or more months with the writers. A lack of previous film experience does not matter to Reed, since he believes that the original author's freedom from formula and involvement in his story are more important than mere technical knowledge of a professional scenarist.

Reed's practice is to shoot his films straight through in sequence, from the beginning to the end. He ordinarily does not begin filming until the script is finished to the last detail, so that he knows exactly where he is going at all times. He was once forced to depart from this method; while directing the 1962 version of

Mutiny on the Bounty, he had to shoot scenes with the script coming from the studio a page or two at a time. Finally released from the picture, he declared that it was impossible to make a film that way.

Graham Greene is a writer with whom Reed collaborated successfully on *The Third Man, The Fallen Idol,* and *Our Man in Havana.* Greene has described the work on *The Third Man:* "On these treatments Carol Reed and I worked closely together, covering so many feet of carpet a day, acting scenes at each other. No third ever joined our conferences; so much value lies in the clear cut-and-thrust of argument between two people."[14] One of the arguments concerned the ending of the film. Greene felt *The Third Man* too light to carry the weight of an unhappy ending and thought few people would wait during Anna's long walk from Harry Lime's graveside past Holly Martins. After seeing how effective was Reed's version of the ending, Greene admitted that he had not given enough consideration to the mastery of Reed's direction or to the zither music of Anton Karas. Sarris has called the scene "one of the most memorable endings ever filmed."[15] It certainly is one of the many examples illustrating the results of Reed's close work with the writer.

If there is a characteristic common to Reed's films it is his use of understatement, his refusal to use technique to exploit emotion or for merely sensational purposes. Reed has long tried for a casual naturalness in his handling of dialogue. He has used the subdued delivery of a crucial speech to build suspense in a number of his films including *Odd Man Out, Our Man in Havana, The Third Man, The Stars Look Down,* and *The Fallen Idol.* He also builds suspense by editing away from climactic moments and by treating human confrontation indirectly. The focus in scenes of violence such as the shooting of Pat and Nolan in *Odd Man Out* is shifted away from the violent act. Instead, as Pat and Nolan are killed, we are shown Teresa, who has sprung the death trap, standing nervously against the door. Tension is heightened by Reed's practice of not underlining the climactic moment but extending the action beyond the moment. A number of examples of this technique are examined in the following analysis of *Odd Man Out.*

4 ·

the production

Odd Man Out was Carol Reed's first project following five years of film work for the military during the Second World War. The technical maturity that Reed gained during the making of such important war films as *The Way Ahead* and *The True Glory* influenced the works that followed. Moreover, Reed had at his disposal at this time some of Britain's best film artists and technicians who had developed during the previous decade as well as the financial backing of men like J. Arthur Rank and Alexander Korda.

Reed's cameraman for *Odd Man Out* was Robert Krasker whom James Agee has called "one of the best cameramen alive."[16] Krasker, a native Australian, has been highly praised for his work on David Lean's *Brief Encounter* (1946) and Laurence Olivier's *Henry V* (1944). After *Odd Man Out,* Krasker joined Reed again to make *The Third Man* for which he won the Academy Award in 1950 for black and white cinematography. Krasker's later credits include *The Quiet American* (1958), *Billy Budd* (1962), and *The Collector* (1965).

Krasker's camera helped to capture the character of Belfast as a night city, the site of Johnny's tortured travels through rain and snow. Reed's work on wartime documentaries led him to join other postwar filmmakers in getting away from the studio. Reed himself sought out locations for shooting *Odd Man Out* in Belfast and spent more than a month filming there. Agee praised the result: "Movies have always been particularly good at appreciating cities at night; but of the night city this is the best image I have seen."[17]

Reed also made use of actual sounds to heighten the feeling of the city. For example, the dull, slow beat of the mill machinery heard during the robbery was recorded at an actual mill. The hoof-beats of the horse pulling the coal wagon which threatens to block the escape of the get-away car was recorded in a street with high buildings. According to Karel Reisz in *The Technique of Film Editing,* the use of any library shot of horses' hoofbeats would have established the presence of the coalcart but recording a deliberate echoing sound on location achieved in the context of the scene a "claustrophobic significance."[18] There are many additional examples of actual sounds recorded on location effectively used in the film.

The music composed by William Alwyn was one of the most distinctive features of *Odd Man Out.* John Huntley praised Alwyn's music as "a supreme study in all that is best in film music."[19] As a professor of composition at the Royal Academy of Music in London, Alwyn had long experimented in methods of developing more integrated scores for film: "I like to read the script and discuss the subject with the director and generally identify myself with the film at its inception. . . . The dramatic impulse should be fresh and the inspiration comes from seeing the film. Film music is visual music."[20] Alwyn emphasized that film music should be judged purely on its relationship to the picture. Alwyn aimed at obtaining a perfect integration of dialogue, sound effects, and music. He commented on the disastrous results when the composer and the sound editor try to achieve the same effects independently and negate one another's work. Alwyn has said that his most satisfactory scores resulted when there was close and intelligent cooperation, as in *Odd Man Out.*[21]

Alwyn had worked with Reed on *The True Glory,* composing a highly emotional score for the joint American and British documentary which recorded the victory of the Allied forces over the Germans on the western front. For *Odd Man Out,* Alwyn composed leitmotifs for Johnny, Kathleen, and Shell. The theme for Johnny's walk was written and recorded before the film went into production and James Mason practiced many hours walking in time to it. During the filming, sections of Alwyn's score were played over a loudspeaker in the studio to evoke the feeling for the scenes about to be shot. Reed directed the final scene of *Odd Man Out* with Alwyn's music in mind. Other important sounds from the sequence, like the chiming of the clock, the ship's horn, and the gun shots, had also been worked out by Reed and Alwyn before the scene was filmed, contrary to usual practice of preparing a musical score after the film is completed. Alwyn achieved a quasi-Irish folksong quality in the score which helped to capture the mood and flavor of the setting without sounding cliched. Such careful integration of music with the dialogue and sound effects succeeded in creating a memorable dramatic score.

In casting *Odd Man Out,* Reed supported his star James Mason with some of the finest actors of Dublin's Abbey Theatre. Mason—who had previously appeared only in British films—was at the peak of his popularity during the filming of *Odd Man Out.* For four consecutive years Mason had been cited by the *Motion Picture Herald* as the male actor who brought the most money to British box offices. During an interview in 1955, Mason said that *Odd Man Out* had remained his favorite picture. Contrasted with Mason, many of the Abbey actors were not well known outside of the Irish theatre.

Kathleen Ryan, who played Kathleen in *Odd Man Out,* was acting in Dublin when discovered by Reed. Her later movie career was brief and undistinguished. Cyril Cusak who played Pat had been acting for the Abbey since 1932: *Odd Man Out* was his British film debut. Cusack, of course, is now one of Ireland's leading stage actors. In 1955, Cusack presented the first performance of Sean O'Casey's *The Bishop's Bonfire* at the Gaiety in Dublin. He most recently played Sam in the American Film Theatre's production of Harold Pinter's *The Homecoming* (1974). Denis O'Dea, the Head Constable, was another Abbey actor who had appeared in John Ford's *The Informer* (1935). Reed would use O'Dea again as Inspector Crowe in *The Fallen Idol.*

The two most famous Abbey actors who added their unique talents to *Odd Man Out* were W. G. Fay as Father Tom and F. J. McCormick as Shell. Fay, who along with his brother Frank J. Fay was one of the founders of the Abbey, was the Abbey's first stage manager and was considered the theatre's first great comic actor. F. J. McCormick was one of the greatest and most versatile of the Abbey actors. McCormick played the role of Seumas Shields in the premiere production of Sean O'Casey's *The Shadow of a Gunman* in 1923. The next year he originated the role of Joxer Daley in *Juno and the Paycock,* playing opposite Barry Fitzgerald's Captain Boyle. During the first production of O'Casey's *The*

Plough and the Stars (1926), McCormick was the spokesman for the actors in trying to quiet the riots that accompanied performances of the play. McCormick has been immortalized in the foyer of Dublin's Peacock Theatre in a portrait titled "The Uncrowned King," which shows him surrounded by cameos of his most famous roles, including that of Shell. McCormick died on April 24, 1947, the day after *Odd Man Out* opened in New York, and was mourned by all of Dublin. The presence of so many Abbey players, whether in major or minor roles, gave a strong sense of ensemble acting in *Odd Man Out.*

Also notable in the cast were Fay Compton, Robert Beatty, and Robert Newton. Fay Compton, whose film career began in 1917, has long been a leading actress on the London stage. She created the title role in J. M. Barrie's *Mary Rose* (1920), played Ophelia in John Gielgud's *Hamlet* in 1939 and Regan in the Old Vic production of *King Lear* in 1940. Robert Beatty's films since *Odd Man Out* include *Captain Horatio Hornblower* (1951), *Man on a Tightrope* (1953), *The Horse's Mouth* (1954), and *2001: A Space Odyssey* (1968). Newton's highly individual acting style made its mark on such roles as Bill Walker in *Major Barbara* (1941); Pistol in *Henry V* (1945), and Bill Sikes in *Oliver Twist* (1948).

Important contributions were made to *Odd Man Out* by Roger Furse and Ralph Brinton. Furse, responsible for production decor on the film, had a long background as a stage designer, especially for the London Old Vic. He was temporarily released from the British Navy in 1944 to design the armor and costumes for Olivier's *Henry V.* After his work on *Odd Man Out,* Furse designed the settings for Olivier's *Hamlet.* Brinton, originally trained as an architectural designer, served as art director for *Odd Man Out.* He had thirteen years experience in British film before working on *Odd Man Out.* His drawings of scenes from *Odd Man Out,* especially the ones showing Lukey's studio, brilliantly capture the world of the film. According to one critic, Furse and Brinton made some of the most convincing impressionist pictures of an Irish City in troubled times.[22]

Odd Man Out was based on a novel of that name by F. L. Green, an Englishman resident in Belfast. Author of a number of other novels, including *Music in the Dark, Give Us the World,* and *The Sound of Winter,* Green had little film experience. *On the Night of the Fire,* his novel about a barber who steals for his wife's sake, was filmed in 1939 with Ralph Richardson and Diana Wynyard.

Reed travelled to Belfast to discuss the project with Green and made him coauthor of the screenplay. Collaborating with Green was R. C. Sherriff, a playwright and screen writer. Sherriff's most famous play was *Journey's End* (1928) written for the Kingston Rowing Club for an amateur presentation. The play was filmed in 1930, directed by James Whale, and made Sherriff, then a building inspector, both rich and famous. He never duplicated his first success but he did work on a number of notable screenplays including *Four Feathers* (1939) and *Goodbye Mr. Chips* (1939).

Reed labored on the *Odd Man Out* project with Sherriff and Green for almost a year with the screenplay going through many versions before it was ready to be filmed.

Despite the number of changes, the transition from novel through several versions to the finished film was not particularly drastic. The film is very much in the spirit of the novel, with many scenes kept practically intact from novel to film. There is a certain inevitable telescoping of events and characters, but most interesting are the places where the material has been amplified or added and the effect of the new material on the film. Such significant additions and expansions will be dealt with in the analysis of *Odd Man Out.*

analysis

Odd Man Out opens with an aerial view of Belfast showing the harbor and the surrounding hills. This panoramic shot serves at once to locate the specific area in which the story will take place and to suggest the greater world—free and open space—to which Johnny wishes to escape. The subsequent action occurs in confined places such as Johnny's room, the air raid shelter, the crib of the Four Winds Public House, and Lukey's studio. The claustrophobic feeling of even the exterior scenes, set during a rainy and then a snowy night, is further emphasized by skillful lighting, which is often low key.

The sense of confinement in both interior and exterior scenes supports the motif of Johnny as prisoner. Johnny has been hiding at Kathleen's house for six months; he hallucinates the air raid shelter into a prison and the girl on the skate into his guard; and he is kept a prisoner by Lukey and Shell and all the other characters who want to use him for their different purposes. The larger view of Belfast is not repeated and contrasts vividly with the limited world in which Johnny—and the rest of the characters—struggle for life.

During the opening shots, titles state the theme of the film:

> The story is told against a background of political unrest in a city of Northern Ireland. It is not concerned with the struggle between the law and an illegal organization, but only with the conflict in the hearts of the people when they become unexpectedly involved.

The prologue was not included in the advance screenplay and seems an unnecessary addition to the film. As if not trusting the story to make the point, the audience is in essence told that the film is more than a thriller about tracking down a political fugitive from an ideological crime.

Two recurring motifs are established in the opening moments

of the film. The first is the use of time which is introduced by shots of the bell tower and the face of the clock indicating 4 o'clock. Time assumes great importance in the film. The characters and the audience are constantly reminded of the passage of time by repeated shots of clocks and especially by the ominous face of the bell tower clock, which dominates the city, and its accompanying bell chimes, which seem to toll Johnny's life away. During the planning of the robbery, the clock chimes are an innocent reminder to Johnny that it is time for tea. *Odd Man Out* ends with a shot of the clock as it strikes midnight, sounding the inevitable death of Johnny.

The second motif is the use of children as indifferent life forces witnessing Johnny's tragic odyssey. The camera cranes down the length of the bell tower and reveals a slum section of Belfast with children playing in the streets. The camera pulls back and Dennis is discovered standing at an open book stall. A sense of apprehension is established by Dennis' movements as he suddenly tosses down a book and hurries along the sidewalk. As he moves toward Kathleen's house, a shot of a little girl crying in a doorway adds to the urgency of the movement. Thus, from the very opening of *Odd Man Out,* time and children begin to play their important parts.

The camera pans with Dennis as he enters Johnny's upstairs room and crosses to his seat. The pan shot, following Dennis past the other characters in the room, gives the sense of his interrupting and then joining the action in progress. This shot is repeated later in the scene, when Kathleen enters with the tea. During the following scene at which the robbery is planned, the room is made to seem crowded by the dominant use of close-up (often with only partial faces in the frame), quick cutting, and frequent angle shots. During most of the scene, Johnny is framed against the window and the outside view of tenements with clothes hanging on lines and smoke coming from chimneys. Also seen are the clouds which foreshadow the rain and snow to follow. The close-up is skillfully used to reveal inner feelings of the characters. For example, shots of the men planning the robbery are juxtaposed with reaction close-ups of Kathleen looking off and listening intently to the proceedings. While Johnny is talking to the gang or just to Dennis, he is seen several times from low angle, emphasizing his dominance. When Johnny is alone with Kathleen, the angles are eye-level, reducing Johnny to "normality." Kathleen's involvement with Johnny is expressed by the intimate use of close-up long before her feelings are revealed by dialogue. In the scene Reed has obtained low-keyed acting, which increases rather than decreases the tension.

Johnny's opposition to violence is expressed several times during the scene. Pat is shown holding his gun fondly and boasting, "Anybody that asks for it can have it." Johnny admonishes Pat, telling him that he has not been mixed up in shootings before and that he should not start now. Moments later, Johnny picks up his own shoulder holster and stares at it. During a quick series of close-ups, Dennis questions Johnny's feelings about the job. Johnny paradoxically goes about the business of putting on his shoulder holster as he speaks against violence: "I believe in everything we're trying to do, but this violence isn't getting us anywhere." Dennis reminds Johnny of his imprisonment for transporting guns and ammunition. Johnny, as he secures the holster about his waist, responds with the speech that establishes his ethical frame of reference: "In prison you have time to think. If only we could throw the guns away and make our cause in the Parliament instead of in the back streets!" Ironically, it is Johnny who will commit the violent act and not Pat, Murphy, or Nolan with all their irresponsible bravado.

There is a struggle between Johnny's newly acquired concern for nonviolence and his sense of responsibility as the leader of the organization. The conflict within Johnny is intensified by implications that he is no longer the man he was. The confrontation is three-cornered: Dennis rightly questions Johnny's ability to lead the assault on the mill and offers to go in his place for the good of the organization, and Kathleen wants Johnny not to go because of her strong feelings toward him. Reed, as is his style, treats the confrontation indirectly. When Dennis challenges Johnny's fitness to lead the raid ("Your heart's not in this job, Johnny"), he is looking away from Johnny, casting a large shadow on the wall. Before the line, Reed has given the actor Robert Beatty the business of rising from a chair and taking off his hat as he turns to the wall. Johnny's first response to Dennis and Kathleen is to say in an almost amused tone, "So I look soft then?" As Dennis pursues the question, Johnny tells him, "Dennis, I'm the leader of the Organization in this city. I've spent months planning this raid to get the funds for all the things we need. For Maureen and her husband and the others. I've got my orders and I'll see them through. When I want your advice, I'll ask for it." As Johnny asserts his authority, he has been putting on his shoe. Rather than undercutting the speech, performing the simple task gives his words more dramatic significance: Johnny breaks his lace while reassuring Kathleen, "It will go fine." The sudden breaking of the shoe lace after Johnny's decision to go to the mill is a premonition of death. This image is repeated in the final scene of the film when Shell breaks his shoe lace before the deaths of Johnny and Kathleen.

The final minutes of the scene as Kathleen helps Johnny get ready are played with much restraint, considering the situation. Johnny does not agree with what he is about to do and yet he must carry out the robbery because it is his duty. Kathleen, whose feelings toward Johnny have been eloquently revealed by Krasker's camera, does not want to lose the man she has come to love. She responds with a wan, uneasy smile. He speaks optimistically about what he will do after the robbery. He lightly asks her whether he looks like a businessman. Kathleen, momentarily distracted by his apparently calm manner, wants to know if Johnny plans to come back to the house. When Johnny answers that he will be hiding in the hills, Kathleen asks if she can see him there. Kathleen obviously feels much more strongly about Johnny than he does about her. Preoccupied with his mission, he thinks of Kathleen as no more than "a great friend." This is an unorthodox love scene and yet a poignant one. Once Johnny leaves the room, the two will not be together until Kathleen finds him in the snow and takes him to his death. A question that Kathleen asks is in this scene, "Johnny, will you ever be free?" echoes through the film and is finally answered by Kathleen herself.

The quiet and desperate mood of Kathleen's farewell to Johnny on the stairs is broken by a sudden dissolve into a pan shot of Pat driving the get-away car down a city street. Alwyn's music skillfully bridges the abrupt change of mood and place. The restraint of the planning gives way to the frantic tempo of the robbery. Contrasted to the scene in Johnny's room, the robbery is purely visual with no reliance on dialogue. However, music and sound are very important to the effectiveness of the scene. Increasing use is made of pan shots and combinations of traveling shots and close moving shots to capture the erratic movement of the car and the feeling of speed. By the time Pat has picked up Johnny at the bookstore, the camera has started to move from objectively recording the passing scene to a subjective view of Johnny's dizziness.

At first, the camera pans with the car and then lets the car pass it. After Johnny has been picked up, there is a close moving shot of a streetcar track passing under the camera followed quickly by a tilting of the camera to the facades of the buildings. Other detail is picked up at random, especially the blurred images of streetcar tracks and cobblestones, as the audience is made to feel the motion which sets off Johnny's dizziness. A low angle shot of a passing streetcar is followed by a large close-up of Johnny's face already showing signs of distress. A traveling shot of buildings at a low angle is followed by a close moving shot of the brick pavement with a bicycle rider passing in the background. A traveling shot of overhead wires is followed by another large close-up of Johnny. A pattern is set of increasingly random images alternating with large close-ups of Johnny more visibly disturbed. Johnny's dizziness is intercut with the wheels of a bus moving in the opposite direction of the camera and a man walking by a sign-covered fence. The camera becomes more and more subjective in recording the dim and distorted world that Johnny sees. A double tension has been created in the scene. Reed and Krasker have carefully constructed the progression of images depicting Johnny's dizziness. They have established that Johnny's self-control in the first scene is fragile. Secondly, added to the inherent dangers of the robbery, the possibility that Johnny might have another attack of dizziness forbodes grave consequences.

The robbery scene offers a good example of the imaginative use of sound in *Odd Man Out*. The sudden stopping of the music as the car pulls up to the mill dramatically begins the sequence. As Johnny, Murphy, and Nolan leave the car, the city clock begins its relentless chiming. An extreme angle shot up to the top of the mill chimney is followed by a close-up of Johnny trying to clear his vision. The chimney belching smoke, first seen during the ride, dwarfs the troubled Johnny like a monster guarding the mill. Krasker's camera achieved the effect requested by Green and Sherriff in the advance screenplay: "This [the mill with its chimney] should be shot in such a way to give the impression that it is leaning forward over Johnny."

Unlike the usual thriller where the success or failure of the robbery is kept in doubt, the sounds of the clock chimes and the image of the mill and its towering chimney are ominous signs that the venture is ill-fated. The hurried movement of Murphy and Nolan, as shot through the glass doors from inside the mill, contrasts with Johnny's efforts to pull himself together before entering the doorway, another indication of his weakness at this crucial moment.

The choice of a mill as the site for the robbery allowed the creative use of sounds made by machinery. In a similar use of machinery sounds at the opening of Fritz Lang's *The Last Will of Dr. Mabuse* (1932), tension is created in a scene where a man, hiding from his potential killers, cowers in fear as the sounds of a printing press become louder and louder. The steady pounding of the machine contrasts with the tensed, quiet nervousness of a concealed man. For *Odd Man Out,* the slow beat of the machinery was recorded on location at a mill. During the robbery, the beat of the mill machinery becomes progressively louder. The persistent mill sounds heard while Johnny, Nolan, and Murphy are hurrying to finish the robbery abruptly stop during the cuts to the waiting Pat, sitting apprehensively in the car. Pat hears the footsteps of two people walking up the mill stairs and involuntarily steps on the accelerator, leaving the motor running during the next shots. In fact, the sounds outside the mill are becoming subjective as Pat's over-sensitivity to everything he hears is revealed by exaggerated volume on the sound track. To Pat even an object with a potential for sound takes on a fearful significance; he seems frightened when the camera pans to the enormous burglar alarm on the mill wall.

Following the shot of the silent alarm bell, the sound of hoof-beats and the cry of a coal man warn Pat of a real danger. A horse-drawn coal cart, shot from Pat's eyeline, slowly approaches, blocking the exit of the get-away car. The revving of the car engine continues as a counterpoint to the sounds of the mill machinery while Pat sits in the car distressed by the appearance of the unexpected obstacle. With both the alarm bell and coal cart established as threats to the success of the robbery, the scene cuts back to the accounts office where Johnny is putting bundles of banknotes into his brief case. Reed has chosen to place Nolan, displaying the same bravado witnessed earlier, at the focal point of the robbery. The image of the alarm has heightened the suggestion that the robbery will be noticed: at any time one of the mill-girls working behind the glass partition could detect the crime and ring the bell. Karel Reisz has pointed out another function of the mill sounds in the scene:

> the dull unhurried beat of the mill stresses the slow passage of time while the men are trying to get the money away. By dividing time, so to speak, into a series of mechanically following units, the rhythmic beat of the mill makes the sequence intolerably long-drawn out, almost as if we were experiencing it through the mind of a member of the gang.[23]

As in the exterior shots involving Pat, little sounds are used subjectively in the mill. The fear of discovery causes the men to hear every sound as if magnified. Incidental noises like the opening of doors, footsteps, the clicking of briefcases, and the rustling of banknotes, all seem excrutiatingly loud. Contrary to natural sound perspective, their footsteps become louder as the men walk down the corridor away from the camera. Nolan's whistling adds to the aural montage of the scene. A few seconds after the men leave the accounts office, the alarm bell is rung. Because of the increased value of insignificant sounds in the scene, the sound of the naturally loud alarm bell takes on an even greater power. The dominant sound in the scene changes from the pulsating rhythm of the machinery to the piercing and persistent ring of the alarm.

Johnny's killing of the clerk is a pivotal incident in the film. It is important that the shooting appear more a desperate accident committed by a confused man than a cold-blooded act of murder. As Johnny leaves the mill, he stops and tries to cover his eyes. During the robbery, Johnny had performed efficiently, not showing the effects of his earlier dizziness. Now, with escape a few feet away, Johnny falters on the steps. A tension is created between Murphy, Nolan, and Pat shouting for Johnny to get into their car and yet powerless to help the dazed Johnny who is unable to move.

The following series of shots emphasize Johnny's distressed state both objectively and subjectively. The shots move from a large close-up of Johnny blinking his eyes at his sudden entry into daylight, to a blurred view as seen by Johnny, to another close-up of Johnny putting his hands over his closed eyes, to a close-up of Johnny's feet feeling for the edge of the step. He appears to be no match for the armed clerk. A series of close-ups records the struggle that follows. The tightness of the shots serves to depict an unheroic struggle between two ill-equipped combatants where all the details are not visible. As one critic has written, "The tussle on the steps of the mill . . . is not a photographic record: the camera seems within the locked bodies of the fighters."[24]

As is his practice throughout the film, Reed has chosen to edit away from the violent act and to record reaction to it. When Johnny is shot by the clerk, the audience sees the reaction of Pat, Murphy, and Nolan sitting helplessly in the car. Johnny is in pain and pulls his own gun, significantly for the first time, from the shoulder holster. When Johnny shoots the clerk, the camera is panning to Nolan and Murphy hurrying from the car. The sequence climaxes not with the shooting but with Johnny's cry of pain, "Look out!" when his wounded arm is clumsily grabbed by his terrified accomplices. The car drives off wildly and we see the motionless body of the clerk, his pistol lying beside him.

An important difference between the novel *Odd Man Out* and the film *Odd Man Out* is that the novel opens with the raid on the mill while most of the opening scene in the film is devoted to planning the robbery. The additional episode is more important to the film's theme than to its plot. For much of the story, the wounded Johnny McQueen is a character acted upon rather than acting. As more and more of his life drains from him, the weakened Johnny is able to be only a passive character, and the focus is placed on the way the other characters react to him. He becomes a touchstone revealing the basic nature of others.

The addition of the opening scene in the film gives Johnny the opportunity to relate actively to the other characters as a person and not merely as a symbol. More important, the opening scene establishes an ethical frame in which Johnny is presented as a moral, sensitive protagonist questioning the values of violent action.

Although he does kill a man, it is not a premeditated murder; he is a murderer-in-spite-of-himself. By establishing such a frame, the question is shifted from Johnny's guilt to the charity in the other characters. This point will be examined in more detail later, but note here the great pains taken to exonerate Johnny from blame for the death of the cashier.

During the next sequence, Murphy and Nolan try desperately to pull Johnny into the car. The sounds made by the car, driven erratically by Pat, add to the tension of the scene. The indelible image of the scene is the figure of the wounded Johnny hanging from the speeding car and at the mercy of three men who have lost their courage and their control. There is a deliberate grotesqueness about the scene as Reed plays with our conflicting responses to add to the sense of nervousness and disorientation. Johnny's fall from the car is the final event of the robbery scene. A large close-up of Johnny losing his grip on the car and falling backward is followed by a close pan shot of Johnny hitting the pavement and rolling. The camera holds Johnny in the center of the frame as it moves away from him.

Music, which has been conspicuously absent from most of the earlier sequences, is dramatically introduced at this point in the film. A loud chord is heard as Johnny hits the ground. All the previous action has served to set the situation. The shot of Johnny falling from the car signals the beginning of his isolated and tragic wanderings. The music continues and is joined by the screeching of the brakes and later by the loud barking of a dog, examples of the skillful use of a combination of music and natural sounds in the film. Reisz correctly described the significance of the introduction of music during the shot: "Because music has been used sparingly to this moment, its sudden entry makes a more precise and definite point than would have been possible with a continuous background score."[25] Alwyn's music, now that it has entered the action with its full dramatic power, becomes a dominant effect for the remainder of the film.

A series of quick shots cuts between Johnny and the car where the men argue what they should do next. Johnny is shown alternately lying helpless on the street, then raising himself, and finally running. Cut into the sequence is a close-up of a white dog, whose barking is dramatically used to accompany Johnny's flight to the air raid shelter. The dog, seen earlier seated on a doorstep, runs barking towards Johnny as if chasing him, symbolic of the pursuit of Johnny during the rest of the film, and follows him out of the frame. There is a sudden shot of Johnny running through the rubble of the bombed out area. A medium high pan shot shows us more of the devastated area as Johnny stumbles over the rubble with his left arm dangling uselessly at his side. The dog, whose barking and apparent following of Johnny have added to the urgency of the flight, surprisingly races ahead of Johnny.

The final moments of the sequence are some of the strongest in the film. Johnny staggers into the air raid shelter. The crunching sounds of the broken glass under his feet and his heavy breathing emphasize his suffering. The distant sound of the alarm is a constant reminder of the robbery. The camera dollies up and pans as Johnny comes forward, his face reflecting his exhaustion. The camera tilts down as Johnny sinks to the floor, his head resting against the wall. The camera moves down for a close-up and we see the startling image of blood running out of his sleeve and over his hand.

During the scenes around the air raid shelter, Reed makes brilliant use of children. Pat, Murphy, and Nolan are vacillating between trying to find Johnny and wanting to leave the area. Pat says, "I'm not going to stay here. It's too bloomin' risky." As the car reaches a side street, Pat tells the others to look for Johnny, but the men see only a group of children playing near an air raid shelter on the deserted street. The use of children becomes more frequent as the scene develops. Johnny's flight is watched by a little girl sitting at an open fire in the rubble.

After Johnny collapses in the air raid shelter, the scene dissolves into a series of shots that record the police's activity. In quick succession, we see a montage of police checking identity cards of men in all parts of the city. With an economy of footage, we are told that there is a massive search for Johnny and that the police are everywhere checking all possible escape routes. The short sequence is all the more telling because it is juxtaposed with shots of the object of the manhunt helplessly lying on the floor of the air raid shelter. Johnny's situation is made more desperate as the quick series of shots dissolve to a map of Belfast, and an impersonal hand draws a circle around the area where he is hiding. The police cordon is complete: evidently there are no avenues of escape.

The map dissolves into a scene showing boys of various ages mocking the policemen as they conduct their search. Throughout the film, gangs of boys parody the life and death struggles taking place. At times, the children serve almost as a Greek chorus alternately commenting on and acting out the incidents of the story. In revealing close-ups, raggedly dressed boys shout comments describing what the police are doing ("They're all lined up to get Johnny McQueen"), offer to find Johnny dead or alive for a share of the reward, or announce the arrival of the chief of the "cops." One boy leaning against a pillar waves an arm and shouts mockingly: "Hey, do you want my identification card?" Another small boy runs to the curb and points a toy gun at the policemen. As his friends scatter, the boy shouts, "I'm Johnny McQueen. I'm Johnny McQueen. All the police are looking for me." Reed has skillfully captured the double-edged qualities of innocence and callousness in the games played by the children; he thus gives an image of a society corrupted by a legacy of hate and conflict—a society at war.

A shy little girl on a single skate, much different in behavior from the rowdy boys of the last scene, figures very prominently in two episodes of *Odd Man Out*. Following a scene in Kathleen's house where Pat, Murphy, and Nolan are accusing each other of losing Johnny, the film returns to the air raid shelter. Again, Reed uses children brilliantly to build the scene. The opening shot is a close-up of Johnny sprawled on the floor. Leaning on a bench, Johnny tries to straighten himself up. Reed uses the exuberant sounds of the children playing off camera to further point Johnny's condition. Two contrasting worlds of carefree abandon and of suffering are set in proximity. They are bridged by a soccer ball inadvertently kicked into the air raid shelter. (The remains of war are ironically used. The "War" is theoretically over, but the war continues.) The girl who retrieves the ball and becomes part of Johnny's hallucination is characterized in a very special way. She is different from the other children. She is also an "odd one out." Without words, she communicates both a fear of Johnny and a compassion for his suffering. She makes such a strong impression in this scene that her later appearance is a startling contrast to the boys begging Dennis for money with their outstretched hands; the boys want "charity," too—the key subject of this film.

The movement from the world of innocent children's games in a cityscape of waste to the subjective world of Johnny's suffering and anxiety is extremely well-handled. Once Johnny is established in the air raid shelter, the camera shows a view of the vacant lot with the boys playing soccer, followed by a close high shot of a boy kicking the ball off the scene. We see the girl with the skate watching as a boy misses the ball. A man walking forward kicks the ball and the girl skates on after it. A pan shot captures the ball's flight as it sails by the tops of the houses. The camera follows the girl as she skates along watching the ball. The kicking and the bouncing of the ball, the scraping of the skate, and the shouting of the children all create a sound background to the action. We become apprehensive as the ball follows an uncanny course towards Johnny's hiding place. We see that Johnny may be discovered by mere chance. Tension is increased as the ball bounces closer and closer to the shelter. The natural sounds give way to Alwyn's music as it bounces into the shelter.

We now see a close-up of the dazed fugitive. The objective view of the children at play dramatically shifts to a subjective experience of Johnny's delirium. Supported by the musical score, a haunting photographic effect turns the air raid shelter into a prison cell and the girl on the skate melts into a guard. The scene is at first blurred as the guard unlocks the door and comes forward. The incongruous sight of the guard picking up the soccer ball could almost be comic if it were not for the strength of the image. Johnny's lines to the hallucinary guard are important:

> Oh, Donald, what a dream I had. What an outing! I dreamt I had escaped from prison. I dreamt I was on a raid robbing a mill—funds for the organization. . . . After we'd done the job and I shot a man . . . yes, I dreamt I shot a man . . . and I couldn't get into the car . . . somehow I couldn't get into it . . . that's right, I was wounded . . . in the left arm . . . I fell off . . . and I got up and ran along streets . . . afraid . . . afraid I'd killed him.

Johnny's vision of the guard is a dramatic device that reveals his extreme psychological tension. He has committed an act odious to a person with his expressed nonviolent feelings. There is a strong wish in Johnny to erase the deed he has committed, to deny the reality of all that has occurred since he escaped from prison: "I hadn't felt so good ever since I escaped from here." By making it all a dream, Johnny is able momentarily to be free from the guilt and pain that gnaws him. However, the figure of the guard changes back to the little girl holding the ball and the bars disappear from the door. Johnny is abruptly returned to his suffering. (Johnny's inner feelings and fantasies during extreme tension are revealed on several occasions by Reed's use of the expressionistic camera.) A close-up of the worried Johnny is followed by a shot of the girl turning quickly and skating out of the shelter. Another close-up communicates Johnny's realization that all he hoped had not happened is, indeed, a fact. With the realization comes the feeling of pain.

Harry Geduld has noted a significant structural progression in *Odd Man Out.* The child is the first of many characters who encounter Johnny and make him a secret "guilty" or "conscience-ridden" part of themselves. Chronologically, Johnny is discovered by a child; a youthful couple, Lenny and Molly; a young man, Dennis; two middle-aged women, Rosie and Maudie; an older man, Gin Jimmy; Shell, perhaps as old or older than Gin Jimmy, and finally Father Tom, the oldest person to encounter him, "finds" his body. Thus the encounters move from childhood to old age (and death).

The camera dollies up close to Johnny as he puts his hand inside his coat to his wound. He coughs and the scene dissolves to the lower room at Kathleen's. The lighting in Kathleen's room sets the somber mood of the scene. Dennis reads from the newspaper that Johnny has killed the clerk. The main action of the scene is Kathleen's bandaging Dennis as a decoy; the police are to think he is the wounded Johnny. (The use of bandages is another important motif in the film.) There are a number of alternate close-ups of Kathleen bandaging Dennis. The composition of the scene resembles the earlier scenes of Kathleen helping Johnny before the robbery, giving the implication that Dennis wishes that he were Johnny, the symbol and head of the Organization. He wanted to go to the mill in Johnny's place and now he is bandaged as the wounded Johnny.

The two here begin their struggle for Johnny. Kathleen wants to go with Dennis to search for Johnny, telling him, "Sooner or later the police will get him. Let me have him until then." Dennis responds: "As long as he lives he'll belong to the Organization." A line from the novel *Odd Man Out* gives a clue to their motives: "Obviously, she loved Johnny perhaps as much as he [Dennis] did but in her woman's way: to possess, to distract; to inveigle from the organization."[26] The fact that Dennis and Kathleen, the two characters who have the closest relationship with Johnny, are so pessimistic about his survival at this early and inconclusive point in the story, indicates the mood of fatalism that dominates the film. Many of the following scenes are filled with strong suggestions that death is inevitable not only for Johnny but also for Pat and Nolan. Dennis' last words as he exits are, "Stay here." There is a close-up of Kathleen, her face expressing her worry. The camera dollies up close to her as she starts to rise and the scene dissolves to Pat, Murphy, and Nolan moving forward on a narrow street.

Along with the chiming of the clock, the passage of time has been dramatized by the masterful use of lighting to record the steady movement from twilight to darkness. Grotesque shadows are cast on walls and wet streets. Lighting and sound combine to increase the tension of the pursuit of Pat, Murphy, and Nolan through the rain-slicked alleys. The music which began during the last moments of the Dennis-Kathleen scene continues to accompany the police search. Footsteps are used subjectively as during the robbery scene. Pat, Murphy, and Nolan try to avoid the policemen who are stopping men and asking to see their identity cards.

One sequence which illustrates Krasker's effective camera work shows a policeman flashing a beam from his light toward the camera. The next shot shows the beam from the flashlight exposing Pat, Murphy, and Nolan who duck and start to run. The chase is on as a medium close shot shows a policeman, standing by his car, run forward as a second policeman gets into the car and pulls away from the curb past the camera. The sounds of a police whistle and a dog barking are added to the music and footsteps as a number of long shots show Pat, Murphy, and Nolan running through the alleys. The camera has placed the audience squarely in the middle of the manhunt. Two details keep the sequence from becoming just another chase. As the three men jump over a fence into a yard, Pat knocks over a garbage can. The camera pans as the men crowd under a shelter. We share the fear of the men as we see a close-up of the garbage can cover noisily rocking back and forth. Close-ups of the garbage can cover alternate with shots of the three men huddled together until Pat lunges onto the cover silencing it as the feet of the police are seen running by outside the fence.

Breaking the tension, the three men run through a house where they suddenly invade the privacy of a startled couple and exit in a brilliant piece of serio-comic counterpoint. After the three men have eluded the police, Pat suggests they go to headquarters, but then rationalizes that Teresa's would be a good place to hide until the coast is clear. In the novel all three men go to Teresa's and are killed outside. In the film, Murphy leaves at the last moment and heads for his mother's. The film is filled with premonitions of disaster. In this case there is no doubt that Pat and Nolan will be killed. Murphy protests going to Teresa's saying, "There'll only be trouble if we go there," and "I don't know she's tricky. I don't trust her." Both assertions prove true. He listens to his own instincts and survives. Pat and Nolan do not listen and die.

Before the men reach Teresa's, Pat slips and falls on the slick cobblestones. As the men walk up Teresa's steps, the clock begins to chime as it did before the robbery. Nolan has premonition of his death when he says, "Steps. Like at the mill." Pat does not want to hear about that and tells Nolan to keep his mouth shut. Pat's weakness of character becomes even more evident during the scene at Teresa's as he tells more than he should concerning Dennis's plans to find Johnny and the fact that the robbery was planned at Kathleen's house.

Although Maureen Delany appears in only one scene, her well-etched portrayal of the oleaginous Teresa is memorable. Delany communicates with a look or a gesture all that is seething beneath Teresa's flesh and folds and gaudy trappings. Without such a controlled and telling performance, the unwitting betrayal of Johnny and his friends by Pat and Nolan would not have been so credible. We first see Teresa's shadow behind the glass of her door as Pat,

Nolan, and Murphy argue whether they can trust her or not. The effect is startling as Teresa slowly opens the door and looks at the men through devious eyes. Once they notice her, Teresa is able to affect good cheer and invites Pat and Nolan into her place. Contrast her behavior here with the way she pushes the men out of the door at the end of the sequence. At the same time, Teresa communicates much that she is involved in and all that she intends to do simply by the way she draws the curtain in front of a group of men who are evidently gambling in another room. A contrast is established between the austere room at Kathleen's and the ostentatious decadence of Teresa's place. The crumbling plaster, the religious statues and pictures, and the sparse furnishings of Kathleen's are an antithesis to the feathers, flowers, striped wallpaper, soft pillows, paintings, and nude pictures at Teresa's. Pat and Nolan, prodded by Teresa, quickly succumb to their surroundings as they compare the expensive liquor they are guzzling to the tea they were given at Kathleen's.

A further contrast is established between the comfort in which Pat and Nolan find themselves and Johnny's present state of suffering. In an example of editing that skillfully underlines the dramatic contrast of the episode, the scene dissolves from Teresa's place as she invites Pat and Nolan, "Come on into the warm and rest yourselves," to a close-up of Johnny in pain in the dark shadows of the bomb shelter.

The brief scene in the bomb shelter which interrupts the "betrayal scene" at Teresa's accomplishes a number of points. Lenny and Molly with their prosaic problem of a reluctant love tryst intrude upon the hiding place of Johnny whose problem is the serious one of survival. At the same time we have a glimpse into the world of an awkward couple trying in their mundane way to achieve a love relationship: a world far removed from the idealism of Johnny whose abstract causes allow no room for such considerations. Johnny's love relationship with Kathleen is unfulfilled.

A tense moment in the scene is Molly's sensing that there is someone else in the shelter and Lenny's lighting of the match. The fact that Lenny immediately recognizes Johnny establishes how well Johnny is known. The incident raises the question, which is answered during the second half of the film, of how a man who is easily recognized even in the shadows of a shelter expects to escape detection. This scene is important also because it introduces the theme of wilful noninvolvement. Molly tells Lenny not to have anything to do with Johnny ("Don't you get mixed up in this"). Later the head constable tells Kathleen, "Keep out of this business." Rosie, Maudie, and Tom, and later, Gin Jimmy, try to extricate themselves from their involvements with Johnny.

The scene builds to a climax as Johnny staggers to the entrance of the shelter. Shooting past the shelter to the street from Johnny's point of view we see children playing hopscotch and other games, another example of the child motif, and then there is another close-up of Johnny in pain, collapsing against the doorway. The scene dissolves into a medium long shot of Dennis looking about and exiting off camera, and finally there is a dissolve back to Teresa's sitting room where Nolan is in the process of telling how Johnny was shot during the robbery. With great economy Johnny's present situation has been established and the action of Teresa prodding information from Nolan and Pat has been progressing during the brief sequence at the bomb shelter. Throughout *Odd Man Out,* Reed sustains several threads of action so that there is a progression not only on camera but also of events not shown. By interrupting a scene or moving to a scene in progress, Reed has been able to condense a great many incidents and pack much information into the film.

The scene builds relentlessly to the deaths of Pat and Nolan. Two striking images of Teresa in the moments before she phones the inspector are her hand reaching into the frame as she pours the liquor into Pat's glass and her adjusting her girdle as she sits on the arm of the chair to turn on the music. (Much detail in this scene would be comic in another situation.) Because the music is from a source within the locale, the radio in Teresa's sitting room, it functions on several levels. On the level of plot, Teresa turns on the music to help mask the phone call to the inspector. The music serves to counterpoint the double sequences of Pat and Nolan debating the character of Teresa as she is exposing them to the police from her phone booth. By using music from within the scene rather than scored for the scene, the level of the sound varies as the scene cuts back and forth from Pat and Nolan, near the source of the music, to Teresa in the phone booth, away from the source of the music. Ironically, the radio music is Schubert's *Unfinished Symphony*. Pat and Nolan are about to have their activities and their lives cut short. Another sound that heightens the tension of the scene is the hanging up of the telephone by Teresa, which startles Pat and Nolan. This detail was taken directly from the novel:

> In the room they heard the single note which the bell emitted when she replaced the receiver. It was louder than the music which purred and slopped unctuously from the radio.
> "Someone is at the street door!" Pat said fearfully.[27]

Reed handles the shooting of the two men in the manner of the earlier scenes of violence. Teresa rushes the men out of her place. She makes another prophetic mention of the steps as the sound of the police driving up is heard. Finding their way blocked, Pat and Nolan have pulled their guns as the scene cuts back to Teresa listening against the door, the picture of a nude girl on the wall behind her. The camera focuses on Teresa as the shots of the men and then the return volley of the police are heard. The camera slowly dollies up to Teresa for a tighter view of her listening. Again, rather than the violent act, we are shown the reaction to it.

In the moments that follow, Reed repeats several of the motifs he has already established. As the camera cuts to a close shot of the bodies of Pat and Nolan lying face down on the street, the now familiar clock chimes are heard. The camera tilts up and we see a boy looking at the bodies. Teresa comes out of the house and pushes the boy aside feigning innocence and sympathy as she joins a mother and another boy. The head constable moves into the scene, pushing people away with his walking stick, and starts to question Teresa. In one of the telling facial reactions which mark Maureen Delany's performance, Teresa communicates to the head constable that she does not want to talk there. As the two move into the house and shut the door, we are left with the image of a boy moving across the frame looking at the bodies as the clock continues to chime and finally Teresa and the constable silhouetted behind the glass door.

In the next scene, Reed makes increased significant use of children. The girl on the skate helps Dennis find Johnny in the air raid shelter. Boys at play reenact the killing of the clerk by Johnny. Although the robbery of the mill and the killing of the clerk were directed by Reed as realistically as possible, here the robbery as acted out by the boys during their grisly game is a romanticized view of the events, with Johnny played as hero. Action has been imagined by the boys to fit their conception of what the robbery must have been like. The first version of the robbery and killing—the actual, realistic—gains more emphasis by the presentation of the second—the imagined, romantic. The children playacting the robbery as they perceive it ironically reminds us of the actual robbery. The further irony is that Johnny McQueen, lionized by the boys as a daring robber outwitting the police, lies close by, his life draining away.

As Dennis enters the scene, his shadow large on the building wall, the sounds of children yelling can be heard. The scene is shot from the point of view of Dennis as onlooker. Two boys are playing with stick guns on the steps, as other ragged children watch. A close shot on the steps shows one boy loudly knocking the gun from the other boy's hand and the two starting to wrestle. Shouts of "I'm Johnny McQueen" are interspersed with sounds of the fight. The two boys are seen as they wrestle on the front steps and fall to the sidewalk. A close shot down to the sidewalk shows them rolling as they fight. Other boys are urging them on with one boy yelling for the obvious favorite of the crowd, "Go on, Johnny. Hit him!" The escape of the robbers is then enacted as two boys pick up one of the fighters and carry him to a wagon. Unlike the panic of Murphy, Nolan, and Pat, the boys act without hesitation, pulling the surrogate Johnny in the wagon as a group of boys follow. The differences between life and game are noted as the boy who played the clerk is helped to his feet by the other boys.

When Dennis comes forward, the boys run down the steps and gather around him. A memorable image of the scene is the hands of the boys waving like tentacles begging for money. Moments before, they were pretending to be Johnny; now they are demanding "charity." The camera shoots up at Dennis as if showing him from the boys' point of view. The difference between child and adult is emphasized by numerous angle shots. Robert Beatty as Dennis skillfully makes the transition from annoyance at the unruly boys following him to a strategy for pulling information out of them. Dennis first uses the ruse of threatening to call the police. One boy tells him there are no police around there, the information that Dennis wanted to hear. The begging image is sustained with a close-up showing the boys stretching out their hands. At times the screen is filled with hands waving under Dennis' face, an image reminiscent of a 1920s expressionistic play or a film such as Lang's *Metropolis* (1926) where children wave their hands seeking aid from Maria during the flood sequence. One boy holds his nose while he speaks and another begs for a "pahny" and then a cigarette.

While Dennis asks his questions and the children beg, a contradiction is set up between the robbery as it happened and the robbery as it is imagined. Dennis tries to find information that will help him locate Johnny. He knows Johnny is wounded and may be dying. The children give him answers related to their romantic view of the robbery. One boy tells Dennis that the police will never find Johnny and another adds that Johnny escaped in a car. Contrast and optimism of the children with the fatal pessimism of the adults. Dennis realizes that the boys are talking about a robbery that has taken place in their imagination and yet he desperately searches for a clue.

In a telling series of shots, Dennis suddenly sees the little girl on the skate and focuses on the girl whose quiet presence and isolation communicate a knowledge beyond that of the rowdy boys. The sequence begins with a large close-up of three boys begging, followed by a close-up of Dennis and a boy. As Dennis speaks he looks off and sees something that distracts him. Shooting across the street, we see the girl wearing one skate standing by the lamp post. Alternate shots between Dennis and the girl dramatize his split attention as he continues to ask about Johnny but is drawn to the solitary figure at the lamp post.

A close-up of the girl is followed by another close-up of Dennis and the boy. Dennis' attention is drawn more and more to the girl. A close-up panning down to the girl's legs shows her wearing the one skate and establishes that she is the one who saw Johnny. Dennis suddenly tosses a handful of coins on the ground for which the boys dive and moves to the girl. The brief scene between Dennis and the girl is a good example of Reed's economy of direction. Krasker's camera and excellent acting condense much drama into a few moments. Dennis senses that the girl knows where Johnny is hiding. He realizes that she may be the only person who can lead him to Johnny in time to save his life. He also realizes that the girl must be spoken to much differently from the boys. The girl wants to tell someone where Johnny is hiding, someone who will help him, but she is not certain whom to trust. Green and Sherriff had given the girl dialogue in the advance screenplay, but the scene is made more effective and the character of the girl more mysterious by omitting any dialogue for her in the film.

The next sequence begins with a shot across the street showing the girl standing behind a lamp post. Dennis moves past the camera and crosses to her. In the staging of the scene, Dennis either squats or kneels in front of her. During the sequence with the boys, Dennis' obvious height difference affected the composition and resulted in a number of low angle shots. In this sequence, Dennis has moved down to be on a level with the girl. The scene is made more intimate by using a number of shots of either Dennis or the girl facing the camera. The sounds of boys shouting in the background serve as a counterpoint to the sequence. Dennis kneels in front of the girl facing the camera and holds up a coin for her. He quietly asks, "Did you see him? Did you? The man?" The little girl is facing the camera and Dennis as she silently looks down at the coin, turns her head slowly, and nods. Dennis looks off and asks, "Where was he?"

At this crucial point, the sound of girls laughing is introduced into the sequence. A medium long shot down the street shows two girls swinging around the lamp post near the air raid shelter. The sequence cuts back to a close-up of Dennis and the girl. Dennis asks her whether Johnny is hiding in a house or in a shelter. She shakes her head and Dennis begins to speak more urgently. He faces the camera as he holds out a coin to her. Contrasted to the eager boys, she does not take the coin immediately. Dennis asks, "Which one? Show me." In spite of her fear, the girl, shown facing the camera, takes the coin and shakes her head. She moves out of the frame abruptly and we hear the distinctive sound of her skate. Dennis, who has been restraining his questions in an effort not to frighten her, suddenly asks several questions: "Take me to it. Come on. Be a good girl and show me. Did the police come and take him away? Did he run away? And the police never came?"

A large close-up of Dennis is seen as he turns to the camera and looks off to where the girl is obviously leading him. Music, which has not been used during this scene, starts and mingles with the sound of the girl's skate. A medium long shot down the street shows the girls playing near the lamp post and Dennis moving past the camera toward the shelter. Again, Reed's masterful direction of children and his dramatic and varied use of them make a strong effect.

Dennis discovers Johnny sitting on the bench in the shelter. We see Johnny from Dennis' point of view pathetically huddled on the bench against the cold, damp wall. Significantly, Johnny's first words to Dennis, spoken as Johnny faces the camera during a close-up of the two, are "Did I kill that man?" Mason's reading of the line communicates the sense that Johnny has thought about nothing else during his suffering in the shelter. The scene is framed by this concern as Johnny asks Dennis the question again before Dennis runs from the shelter to decoy the police. Rather than an answer to the question, there is an abrupt change of mood from the quiet and desperate urgency of the dialogue between Johnny and Dennis to the sounds of footsteps, police whistles, motors, and the music underscoring the pursuit of Dennis by the police. Johnny's isolation is compounded by his not knowing for certain if he has killed the clerk. Dennis will not answer his questions and in a later scene Rosie and Maudie will not tell him. Johnny carries the uncertainty of his guilt until he overhears Tom state the fact.

The heroic acrobatics of Dennis as he tries to draw the police away from Johnny's hiding place seem quite uncharacteristic of *Odd Man Out*. To have Dennis climb ladders, swing on scaffolding, and leap across roof tops appears incongruous on the surface in a film where human confrontation is treated indirectly and where action is more metaphysical than physical. However, this chase sequence terminates one of the film's major movements. The acrobatics are, in retrospect, the conclusion (and fittingly the climax) of the frenzied pursuits of the gang. *Odd Man Out* can now move on the metaphysical level. Furthermore, if Dennis is seen as a foil to Johnny, the pursuit sequence is important.

As Dennis runs from the police, there are four close-ups of people who do not want to be part of what is happening outside their houses: a woman holding a baby moves behind a curtain, another woman shuts a door, a woman wearing a black shawl steps back into her house, and two old women look up blankly. These shots cutting into the scene have Dennis experiencing people retreating from involvement with a human problem and foreshadow in miniature of some of the reactions to Johnny during his wanderings. As noted above, this motif began with Lenny and Molly in the shelter. In contrast to Dennis, Johnny is incapable of daring physical feats during the chase and later in the struggle on the tram. Once Dennis gives the signal, Johnny is barely able to move from the shelter. In a revealing pair of shots, Johnny is shown nearly falling as he walks unsteadily down a flight of steps. There is an immediate dissolve to Dennis quickly hurrying down another flight of steps. And yet in a film marked by a strong sense of fatalism, Dennis, for all his physical prowess, is captured by the police. A key to his capture are the bandages he has used to impersonate Johnny. The bandages function both as a symbol of Johnny's wound and another of the impersonal forces, along with the barking dog, which trap a person, however great his skills and strength.

The theme that Alwyn wrote for Johnny accompanies him as he leaves the shelter, walking uncertainly across the dark streets. Johnny's wanderings begin the second part of *Odd Man Out*.

During the second part of the film, there is a double movement of people searching for Johnny and people accidentally finding him. Under the category of the searchers fall Kathleen, Dennis, the head constable, Father Tom, Shell, and Lukey. Each of them want something of Johnny. Simply stated, Kathleen wants his love, if only for a few seconds before their death; Dennis wants to save Johnny for the Organization and to prove his own capacity for heroic action; the head constable, representing all of the forces of the law, wants to bring Johnny to justice; Father Tom wants to save Johnny's soul; Shell first wants money for Johnny and then the intangible "faith" promised to him by Father Tom; Tober wants to patch up his body; and Lukey wants to paint a man on the threshold of death. For each character who searches for Johnny, there is a character who unwillingly finds him and wants to get rid of him. Tom discovers Johnny in his house after Rosie and Maudie have tried to help him; soldiers put Johnny, who they think is drunk, in Gin Jimmy's cab; Johnny wanders into a crib in Fencie's Four Winds Saloon.

To Tom, Gin Jimmy, and Fencie, Johnny represents a threat to safety and security. Because of the contradictory motives of the characters, Johnny is kicked about Belfast, as Agee described it, like a deflated football. The fact that Johnny has little control over his journey, that he is almost totally at the mercy of those whose paths he happens to cross gives added significance to his declamation of the passage from St. Paul's *Epistle to the Corinthians* (1:13) in Lukey's studio: "Though I speak with the tongues of man and angels, and have not Charity, I am as sounding brass or a tinkling cymbal. And though I have the gift of prophecy and understand all mysteries and all knowledge, and though I have all faith so that I could remove mountains and have not Charity, I am nothing." Even his life is in the hands of others; Tober, Maudie, and Rosie prolong Johnny's life with their varying medical skills. Kathleen ends it by forcing the police to shoot them.

Despite his weakened condition, Johnny is able to observe what people say about him and do to him. The camera never lets us forget that Johnny knows what is happening. His situation is all the more tragic because he is aware, and yet powerless to help himself. Johnny, in his helplessness, becomes a barometer measuring the basic and base instincts of man. Thus the characters in the film can be examined in light of the charity they show Johnny. In *Odd Man Out,* the suffering of man is very much related to man's charity towards man.

Rosie and Maudie are the first persons whom Johnny meets; the two, especially Rosie, are probably the most sympathetic that he will encounter. Because much of the second part of *Odd Man Out* comes close to allegory, there is a danger that the characters Johnny meets could function only as symbols. Reed has not let this happen. His direction of actors is evident in the scene with Rosie and Maudie as Fay Compton and Beryl Measor create well defined characters in their one appearance in the film. There is a combination of human comedy, frailty, and compassion in their characterizations.

Perhaps because the story of Johnny's wanderings and death is tragic, many critics have overlooked the amount of humor in *Odd Man Out*. The humor is the result of the richness of character detail and serves as a momentary release from the suffering in the film. With few exceptions, Reed is able to keep the delicate balance of the humorous detail and the tragic theme. For example, Rosie and Maudie's arguing whether Johnny's arm is broken or Maudie's concern about Rosie cutting Johnny's jacket are details that help to define the characters. The amount of character humor does not alter the dominantly serious mood.

Because Johnny is so well known, it is important that Rosie and Maudie, evidently war evacuees from England, are established as new to the city. They respond immediately to help a man who they think has been hit by a lorry. In an interesting series of shots, the audience's point of view is different from the character's point of view. There is no doubt that Johnny has not been hit, but Rosie and Maudie view the episode from a different angle. In the final moments of the sequence, there is a traveling shot from the front of the lorry as it drives toward Johnny, who steps back, followed by a close shot of Johnny standing in the center of the street as the lorry speeds past him and exits. The camera tilts down as Johnny falls to the street and there is a close reaction shot of Maudie and Rosie who think Johnny has been hit. In the final shot, Johnny is shown lying near the camera as Rosie and Maudie run towards him closing their umbrellas.

The following sequence is a good example of humor used to define character relationships in a scene which is quite serious. Rosie is established as the more authoritative and Maudie as the follower, the more impressionable. When Maudie insists that Johnny's arm is broken, Rosie tells her not to be so dramatic and to keep calm. As Rosie gives such orders as to get the boiling water, she reminds Maudie that she has failed her "practicals," implying that Maudie is not qualified to question Rosie's judgments. Maudie's reaction to Rosie's concern for germs is "Oh, fuss, fuss, fuss!"

One of the most striking sequences of the scene occurs later in the house as Tom, Rosie's husband, demands to know who Johnny is. There is a close-up of Tom shot from a low camera. The shot is held longer than expected and there is a cut to Johnny's gun lying on a white cloth. There is another close-up of Tom as he exits past the camera exposing Rosie and Maudie framed in the doorway. The camera dollies up to Rosie and Maudie who stand in tableau almost as statues. The sequence's excellent composition and camera work reveal the emotions of the characters with a few deft strokes.

During the ensuing argument among Rosie, Maudie, and Tom, we are not shown the characters who are speaking but the scene is shot from the point of view of Johnny who listens to the words spoken. Johnny overhears from Tom what no one would tell him, the fact that he has killed a man. This is an important moment in the film. The sequence foreshadows a later scene when Johnny hears Tober, Lukey, and Shell arguing over him in Lukey's studio.

As Tom rails against Johnny from the kitchen, Johnny struggles to stand. Krasker's camera seems to be inside Johnny's body feeling all of his pain as it follows Johnny to his feet. The low camera is tilted at an extreme angle, recording Johnny's reaction to Tom's words about "the decent man he killed." Krasker has photographed Johnny during this moment of painful discovery from such an extreme angle that a reflection of the window on the ceiling is clearly seen.

Tom's shifting reactions to Johnny are important to note. When Tom opens the front door, Maudie asks, "What'll Tom do?" Rosie responds, "Tom'll do his duty. He'll go to the police, not thinking of the reward or anything." Rosie's last comment is ironic and is echoed by Maudie who says that Tom will put himself in the way of getting it. When Tom sees Johnny and recognizes him, he is angry at the women for keeping him there. He says that he respects the law and has no pity for men who murder innocent men at their work. But when Johnny leaves, Tom gives him some brandy, a small act of compassion that takes the place of his expected duty of reporting Johnny to the police.

Johnny decides not to be a further burden to Rosie: "Open the door and I'll go out and never trouble you again." An exaggerated use of sound emphasizes the extreme wind as Johnny exits into what is now a pouring rain. Further kindness is shown Johnny as Maudie puts a cap on his head and wishes him luck. Such consideration will be infrequent in the scenes to follow. (In the novel, Maudie has a husband, Sammy, who is also sympathetic to Johnny.) However, Johnny, with the added burden of discovering that he has killed, walks into the stormy night. The clock that has been chiming away Johnny's life is now joined by the weather as another force added to Johnny's suffering.

There is no doubt that the weather has become a character in the film as Krasker's camera lingers on Johnny standing in the rain trying to open the door of a cab. The photography, lighting, and editing combine to make the audience feel the very wetness of the scene and something of Johnny's discomfort as he seeks a refuge from the driving rain. The abrupt entrance of three soldiers trying to catch their bus is used effectively by Reed. For a moment, there is the concern whether Johnny will be recognized and captured by the soldiers. However, this apprehension is quickly dispelled as one of the soldiers, Harry, wants to help Johnny. In an excellent example of the use of sound levels to support the depth of camera field, the soldiers shout back and forth to one another, asking whether Johnny is hurt or drunk. Harry, smelling the brandy, thinks Johnny is "tight" and puts him in the cab. (This is another ironic use of detail. A number of times in the film, Johnny is given something to drink. In subsequent scenes, the smell of liquor on Johnny's breath leads people to believe his unsteadiness is caused by intoxication.) Harry shows Johnny a kindness as he starts him on his aimless journey.

The now familiar clock chimes mark the entrance of Gin Jimmy who will unsuspectingly drive Johnny through the police cordon. With the economy that makes *Odd Man Out* such a rich film, Gin Jimmy is quickly characterized as he goes through the seemingly meaningless task of brushing off his large flower as the rain falls on him. This act is made all the more telling by two close shots of Gin Jimmy through the cab window. A haunting glimpse of Johnny's face, just barely visible through the window, is seen before the ironic exchange between the policeman and Gin Jimmy who weakly jokes that he has Johnny in the back. As the cab drives through the blockade, the scene moves to Kathleen's house, the rain-slicked streets reflecting the street lights dissolve to a shot of Kathleen sitting at a table on which is a lamp that will dominate the following scene.

There are two important confrontations that follow: the first and most obvious is between Kathleen and the constable and the second, the significance of which could easily be overlooked, is between Kathleen and Granny. As dissimilar as the two parts of the scene appear, there is a common thread between them; however different their methods of argument, both the constable and Granny are trying to persuade Kathleen not to look for Johnny. The way in which the two parts of the scene are photographed dramatically contrast the characters of the constable and Granny. During the constable's interrogation of Kathleen the camera is as static as during any scene in the film. A low angle shot of Kathleen seated and the constable standing is held for eighty-three seconds. The constable is characterized almost as a machine-like allegory of the "law" as he questions Kathleen, propping her head back with his walking stick and demanding to know "the truth." His declaration that Johnny belongs to the law now has the ring of a line from a morality play where the principal character's body and soul become the center of a struggle among opposing forces. As if to emphasize that the constable is a machine in human guise, the lamp, an inanimate object, takes on an almost human presence as it attracts focus on the table. At one point in the scene, there is a merging of the inanimate and the animate as the constable walks behind the lamp and for a moment his face and the lamp become one.

One of the tense sections of the scene is the hiding of the revolver. After Kathleen has successfully given the revolver to Granny, the constable tells the policeman, who has been searching upstairs, to look in the room. A close high shot of the room shows Granny watching the policeman. The camera tilts up as the policeman tells Granny to stand up. He finds a bag of sweets in the chair which Granny takes back from him, "Give 'em to me. Them's my sweets." A close-up of Kathleen, looking off anxiously, is followed by another close-up of Granny's crossed hands showing the barrel of the revolver protruding from her sleeve. Suspense is created as we are concerned whether the constable will discover the revolver before Kathleen is able to conceal it again. There is a close-up of the room as Kathleen kneels before Granny and looks at the gun. This shot is followed by a close-up of Granny's hands which close over its barrel, hiding it safely from the constable's view as he now focuses on the roll of bandages he finds.

The camera becomes lyrical during the scene as Granny tells her past life in order to persuade Kathleen not to look for Johnny. The contrasting sections are linked as Granny says of the constable, "That wasn't a bad fellow, as them fellows go. He spoke fair." Considering what has happened before, the line seems surprising. One would not have expected Granny to be sympathetic to the sentiments of the constable. She turns down Kathleen's request for the revolver three times, adding, "There was decency in him. He spoke sense." Granny offers her own life as an example of what Kathleen should do: "Stay here, darlin'—sure, where's the sense in runnin' towards trouble when you know you can't mend it." Granny is one of the most positive persons in a film filled with fatalistic quests. In fact, the two oldest characters in the film, Granny and Father Tom, are the most positive. As sensitively portrayed by Kitty Kirwan, Granny's allegiances are more with life than with causes.

While Granny tells the story of her life, there is a stunning combination of shots which first shows a close-up photograph of Granny on her wedding day. Then, as if the present has intruded on the past, the shadow of her pointed finger is seen on the picture. Finally the camera pulls back and tilts up to a mirror in which Kathleen's face is reflected. The shot is held as if showing Kathleen weighing the alternatives. The comparison between the picture of the young bride and Kathleen's image in the mirror is further pointed by Granny's lines off camera, "That was me on my weddin' day. I was nineteen then and as lovely as yourself." She tells a story about Hughie Fitzpatrick, also a gunman on the run who urged Granny to go with him, that is very much the same as that of Kathleen and Johnny, with the exception that Granny chose not to look for her man. She stayed and "had her life." As Granny falls asleep in the middle of her memories, the choice that Kathleen has made is apparent as she takes the revolver from Granny's sleeve. As she bends over to take the revolver, Alwyn's music, which quietly has used winds and strings to underscore Granny's meaningful nostalgia, suddenly becomes more threatening and urgent.

As the scene dissolves to a medium long shot of Gin Jimmy unknowingly transporting Johnny through the rainy streets, a structural rhythm of *Odd Man Out* has been established. The film will move from scenes of persons looking for Johnny to scenes of Johnny's aimless wanderings. Momentum is gained by the increasing numbers of persons who, with different motives, will join the search for Johnny. The suspense which has been created by the question, "Will Johnny be found?" has gradually shifted to the question, "Who will find Johnny?" To compound this dramatic thrust, two of the key searchers—Shell and Father Tom—have not been introduced even at this late stage.

A number of motifs have been firmly established: We are made conscious of time passing not only by the chiming from the bell tower but also by the increasing view of clocks of all kinds in almost every scene. A clock is very evident during the questioning of Kathleen by the constable. Because time looms so important in the life and death of Johnny McQueen, it can be said that *Odd Man Out* is a film filled with clocks. In the previous scene, bandages continue their importance as they are first shown by a close-up, then hidden by Kathleen, and finally found by the constable. The weather turning from rain to snow will dramatically underscore the increased suffering and approach to death in the latter part of the film.

The section of the film that follows the scene in Kathleen's house is composed of much shorter sequences. The frequent movement from scene to scene heightens the urgency of Kathleen's search for Johnny, her being followed by the police, and Johnny's increasingly desperate situation. More of the city at night, so praised by Agee, is shown as Kathleen moves through the busy streets to the harbor to arrange an escape by sea for Johnny, to a dance hall in an unsuccessful try to elude the police, and finally to Father Tom's. A counter movement occurs as Gin Jimmy continues to drive Johnny through the city, discovers his unwanted passenger, and takes Johnny to a junk yard where he abandons him in a small tub.

Reed uses the clock chimes not only symbolically to toll Johnny's life away but also to establish that action is occurring simultaneously in different parts of the city. When Gin Jimmy pulls Johnny from the cab at the junk yard, the tower, which can be seen in the background, is chiming eight o'clock. When Kathleen is talking to the seaman on the docks, the clock is also chiming eight. The urgency of time is further emphasized as the seaman tells Kathleen that he sails at eleven. Kathleen realizes that she has only three hours to find Johnny and bring him to the ship.

Johnny's decline is made more evident in the junk yard scene as Gin Jimmy, one of the many characters who does not want to be involved in Johnny's problems ("I'm not for you, I'm not against you"), drops Johnny in the mud in his eagerness to get rid of him. Johnny is seen lying almost unconscious in the cab as Gin Jimmy opens the door. A shot of Johnny falling from the frame is quickly followed by a close-up of Johnny in the mud. We are then shown Gin Jimmy dragging Johnny through the junk yard, knocking over the tub where Johnny will be placed. The depth to which Johnny has fallen is dramatized by the image of him lying in the tub as if he were another piece of junk in the yard.

The junk yard scene is notable for the introduction of Shell. The junk yard itself with its random collection of objects foreshadows the fantastic milieu of the house and studio where Shell, Lukey, and Tober live. Reed skillfully builds to the first appearance of Shell. Once Gin Jimmy places Johnny in the tub, the camera moves down close as Gin Jimmy pleads with the motionless Johnny not to tell the police he helped him but to make sure the Organization knows. Gin Jimmy exits from the frame as the camera holds on Johnny lying in the tub, an oncoming train mournfully sounding in the background.

The camera then shoots past the front of the cab as Gin Jimmy is seen scurrying through the junk yard, the train passing behind him. Gin Jimmy comes forward to the cab, climbs onto his seat, and looks down startled. What has Gin Jimmy seen? This is immediately answered as the scene cuts to a close-up view shot down at an extreme angle showing Shell, his derby shining in the night rain, standing in the mud and looking up at the camera. Significantly, the first shot of Shell is a reductive one from a high angle looking down. The early shots of Johnny in Kathleen's house were from a low angle. His first incriminating words, "I saw you, Gin," set the tone for his character and so alarm Gin Jimmy that he quickly leaves. What follows is an almost grotesque dance by Shell as he tries to make up his mind what he should do next.

The theme that Alwyn composed for Shell is introduced during the sequence and brilliantly underscores the actions of the character. Shell looks around in several directions, puts his hands behind his back, scratches his ear, moves unsteadily behind a lamp post, and finally goes into the junk yard where he sees Johnny lying in the tub surrounded by the many objects shown more explicitly in this shot than in the earlier views of the yard. A plaster of paris angel looms up behind Shell as if looking over the affairs of man. The angel is one of the many theological symbols crowded into the second part of *Odd Man Out*. Shell runs from the junk yard, his destination or purpose not for the moment apparent. However, Reed has now set in motion a meeting between Shell, who carries the knowledge of Johnny's whereabouts, and Kathleen, who is desperately searching for him, at Father Tom's.

The following scenes focus on Kathleen as she walks through the crowds past vigilant police to the docks to arrange an escape for Johnny. She is followed by the constable and his detective and, during one sequence (another example of the dramatic use of sound in the film), she tries to lose the detective by slipping through a dance hall. Reed uses a traveling shot of Kathleen walking quickly down a street. The camera holds on the front of the dance hall as Kathleen walks up the steps and into the building. There is a sudden cut to a close-up which reads "No Jitterbugging." The abrupt cut and the contrast in sound from the quiet footsteps and automobile horns to the blaring sound of the band heightens the feeeling that Kathleen has entered a strange world. As the camera tilts down to the jitterbugging couples on the dance floor, there is something incongruous about Kathleen's presence, especially when a sailor grabs her and tries to dance. What is normal, boistrous enjoyment for everyone on the dance floor seems out of place for Kathleen and a little jarring for the audience now involved with the characters in the film. When Kathleen walks back out into the night and shuts the door behind her, the loud sound stops as suddenly as it was introduced. But the sequence is not complete. When Kathleen thinks she has eluded the detective and slows her walk, the sound of the "jitterbugging" is momentarily heard again until the door slams shut. The sounds have told Kathleen that she has not lost the detective. As the constable had earlier, the detective tries to persuade Kathleen not to look for Johnny. His final words before Kathleen enters Father Tom's are another echo of the fatalism in the film, "But you're too late, miss."

A problem with the Father Tom scene, other than the unbroken ten minutes of its length, is that the dialogue is more narrative than dramatic. The adaptation here has not made the transition smoothly from novel to film. The allegory suddenly becomes a little too obvious and, at times, obtrusive as the scene sometimes becomes a debate between Faith and Love. The characters talk too much about hidden feelings and motives and intentions. This is somewhat prepared. for by the symbolic representation of Shell's wounded budgy as Johnny. F. J. McCormick's finely realized characterization of Shell does give the first half of the scene a vitality that keeps the story from losing its momentum, but the film is more effective when the characters are less abstract.

From the very moment Kathleen enters Father Tom's, there is an inevitability about the tragic events that will follow. Father Tom greets Kathleen as if she were predestined to come: "You came to ask me about Johnny McQueen." Realistically, a parish priest would receive a number of visitors; Kathleen could have come for various reasons. But at this point, Father Tom is not just a typical parish priest. Early in the conversation with Kathleen, he reveals that he taught Johnny as a child. This information is important for the understanding of the later scene in Lukey's studio when Johnny hallucinates the image of Father Tom.

The first part of the scene is involved with the story of Shell's "wounded" bird. Reed has given Shell another effective entrance. The very moment Father Tom mentions Johnny McQueen, Shell, who had been sitting out of sight next to the fireplace, leans into the frame. The scene builds as Shell, his bent derby on the cage, tells about his bird. Kathleen, who has come for more important business, is both bored and irritated by the story ("It's a budgy. There are thousands of them"). It becomes increasingly obvious that the story of the bird is a weakly disguised account of Johnny's situation. The audience, who knows that Shell saw Johnny in the tub, makes this discovery before Kathleen. She is impatiently looking out the window, the ever present clock in the background, when Shell mentions that "this fellow is a chief." Kathleen turns to the camera and begins to question Shell. The chimes sound as Shell tells Kathleen the bird's name is Johnny.

Once it has been established that Shell knows where Johnny is —that the cage refers to prison and corner refers to where Johnny is lying—Shell begins to bargain for Johnny's return. At first Kathleen presses him for information, but just as the scene appears to be building, it takes an odd turn and becomes a long discussion between Shell and Father Tom about temporal and spiritual riches. (Shell says he could get a thousand pounds for Johnny, that is, from the police. But he chooses not to. He wants to sell his "bird" to other customers. He expects to profit without being an informer.)

Rather than offer money, Father Tom tells Shell he will try to inspire in him "a precious particle of faith." The priest tries to raise Shell's concerns from pints of stout to higher rewards while Shell wants to know the value of faith in hard cash.

The character of Shell vacillates between shrewdness and naivete. He later bargains skillfully with Gin Jimmy and Fencie. He devises the story of the bird for Father Tom and uses the allegory many times in subsequent scenes. However, he is baffled by the discussion of "faith" and its "worth." He seems unable to grasp spiritual concepts, but he does understand man on earth.

The discussion with Father Tom is important to the film thematically and it is returned to later in a scene between Shell and Tober. However, Reed has chosen a number of close-ups of Shell and Father Tom and, either intentionally or unintentionally, excluded Kathleen from the sequence. The direction is not as imaginative here as in the rest of the film. Shots are held too long and they lack variety. The sequence is composed of alternate close-ups with either Father Tom facing Shell and the camera or Shell facing the camera and Father Tom. Kathleen, who has much at stake here, is not seen for long stretches of dialogue. A very few reaction shots, so important earlier, are used in the sequence. For a time, the film becomes, in Hitchcock's phrase, "photographs of people talking."

After Shell leaves to recover Johnny, Father Tom and Kathleen continue the theological debate. The dominant shot in the sequence is the close-up, often very tight, alternated between Kathleen and Father Tom as they reveal their feelings about Johnny. Father Tom wants to hear his confession and to comfort his soul. He also feels that Johnny must pay for his sins. Kathleen wants Johnny herself, to save him from execution. She says that she would take Johnny's life rather than allow him to be captured by the police and her own life as well. Father Tom tries to tell her that this life is nothing but a trial for the life to come. At one point, he exclaims, "Where's your faith?" Kathleen replies that her faith is her love. Later when Shell asks Tober "What is it—Faith?" Tober replies it is life. In *Odd Man Out* faith equals life/love.

The sermons of Father Tom, all his talk of faith and the life to come, fall on deaf ears: Kathleen does not listen to him and Johnny cannot. Kathleen says that what she feels is stronger than her religion, stronger than herself. Her conviction is evident in her last words to Father Tom, "I believe that what I intend to do is good."

Rain has turned to snow as the scene slowly dissolves to the junk yard where Johnny, the object of contention in the previous scene, remains lying in the tub. The dissolve is made effective by contrasting the subdued tones of the conversation between Father Tom and Kathleen with the sudden blast of the whistle as a train speeds by in the background. Krasker's camera again seems to be inside Johnny as the series of shots that follow reveals the extent of Johnny's suffering and the effort required for him to move from the junk yard. The camera tilts down, as if following the course of the falling snow, and discovers Johnny lying in the middle of the junk. There is a cut to a close-up which is held long enough to show him trying to stand. Music is introduced at this point and it poignantly expresses his state. As the tub topples, he is thrown to the ground with a resounding crash. The sound is exaggerated to express subjectively his pain. The camera tilts up with him as he pulls himself to his feet. A shot of Johnny staggering through the junk yard, the plaster of paris angel prominently at his side, is followed by a close-up of his feet on the muddy ground. The camera follows his exit from the junk yard and in the background can be seen a phone booth where two girls are talking. As Johnny walks toward them, the snow seems to be falling harder and the tower clock looms up behind him like an unfriendly eye.

The phone booth sequence arouses hope and then dashes it. If the phone booth were empty, Johnny might save himself. But it is not and Johnny must keep moving as he sees two policemen. In a telling shot, the camera dollies up close to the booth and we see the girls briefly glance at Johnny walking away as they continue their trivial conversation.

Johnny's theme is heard as he walks along the snowy street. The bandage leitmotif is reiterated as a close-moving shot shows Johnny unwrapping his dressings. They are blowing in the wind as Johnny, alarmed by the sight of two more police, moves toward the entrance of the saloon. When he exits from the frame into the saloon, a piece of the bandage trails after him. Once he enters the saloon, the music stops and is replaced by the conversation and activity of the patrons. The camera records his unobtrusive entrance and pans as, in the background, he staggers into a crib. There is a cut to a close-up of the publican, Fencie, and his barmen who have noticed Johnny. Again, he is an unwanted guest who will be cast out into the storm. A shot of the interior of the crib reveals Johnny slumped on the table. The publican roughly pulls Johnny up by the collar and tries to force him to drink. Johnny's words are barely audible as he tells Fencie he needs to stay and rest. Contrasted are the patrons of the saloon who are drinking and talking boisterously and Johnny who, known to only Fencie and his waiters, sits slumped in their midst.

The clock chimes are sounding as the scene dissolves to Shell running across a street toward a tenement house. The next series of shots reveals the interior of the house in all its fantastic unreality. When the camera shoots down the stairs to show Shell enter through the front door, we are conscious that the film has moved further away from realism. In the earlier scenes Reed has taken meticulous care in location shooting to create a believable environment. Now, however, the interior of the house is obviously a theatrical setting with the stairs, bannisters, pillars, and grotesque shadows creating an almost impressionistic effect that is intensified by snow falling from the dome in the hall ceiling. Later shots of Shell's bird-filled room and Lukey's studio with its high ceilings and wrinkled canvas reinforce this effect.

Lukey and Tober, the two men who share this strange place with Shell, are introduced in the scene. Lukey is first seen in his studio as Shell tries to sneak past him. Robert Newton's characterization of Lukey is as excessive as the settings around him. For much of the scene he is threatening Shell or dragging him about by his scarf. Newton's performance, more than anyone else's in the film, received harsh treatment by the critics. In defense, it can be argued that Newton's ravings and rantings are in harmony with his role and with the thematic progression of the film. Newton's Lukey dramatically contrasts with the exquisite, bird-like performance of McCormick's Shell and Elwyn Brook Jones' enigmatic Tober.

As with Shell, Reed has given Tober an entrance which immediately draws attention to his character. The camera follows Shell who slips away from Lukey and runs from the studio with Lukey following. Lukey has been trying to force Shell to bring Johnny to the house as a subject for him to paint. There is a cut to the hall and Shell is shown running down the stairs as Tober slowly walks up them. One is at first surprised to see another character, whose appearance is announced only by the sound of the wind in the house. Tober continues to walk slowly up the stairs toward the camera paying no attention to the exchange of words between Lukey and Shell. There is a cut to a low camera shot of Lukey sitting by the stove and Tober walking through the door. During the next series of shots, the camera, which has explicitly revealed Shell and Lukey, avoids a clear shot of Tober. As Lukey and Tober talk about the faces in the fire, the smoke covering Lukey's own face, Tober's arm extends into the frame placing a bag on the stove. The shot is repeated as Tober is shown placing a coin in Lukey's hand. Tober, the last major character to appear in the film, has been introduced indirectly.

There are several thematic points raised in the argument between Lukey and Shell. Lukey forces Shell against his will to pose for him. The frustrated Shell desperately wants to return to find Johnny without revealing his intentions to Lukey. When it seems that there is no alternative, Shell does tell Lukey that he knows where Johnny is hiding. As Shell sits for the painting, Lukey declares that he is gaining a kind of immortality: "One day, you'll die, Shell, but this picture will live." Ironically Lukey has chosen to paint Shell as a St. Francis of Assisi–like monk looking angelically towards heaven, Shell posing in the chair where Johnny will later sit. When Lukey discovers what Shell is going to do with Johnny, he acts outraged: "I'm going to hit you hard for trying to sell a man who's on the run." But Lukey is an obvious hypocrite who wants Johnny for his own purposes.

The dying Johnny is scrapped over like a bag of fish and chips. Shell is still obsessed by the "particle of something very precious" he will receive in return for Johnny. Lukey feels that if he could only paint a head and shoulders of Johnny, there would be something in his eyes that would make up for all his failures. When Shell eludes Lukey and runs to find Johnny in the junk yard, it is the disappointed Lukey who goes to Johnny's new resting place as the result of the coin Tober gives him to buy a drink.

The consummate skill of McCormick in communicating depths of feeling with his body as well as his voice is evident in the brief scene in the junk yard. Shell's theme is introduced along with the sound of the train as the junk yard is seen from the street, with the clock in the background. Shell's movements from a dignified caution to a sudden, eager dash into the yard sets up his profound disappointment when he discovers Johnny gone. A closer view of the yard is followed by a shot of Shell's horrified reaction to the empty tub which is then shown in close-up. The striking image of Shell staring at the tub is heightened by the presence of the plaster of paris angel, now with an icicle formed on its face. The camera tilts and pans as it follows Shell's desperate search in the yard for Johnny. The music quietly captures Shell's mood of despair as he crosses the street. In a comic-balletic sequence reminiscent of Chaplin or Keaton, Shell twists and spins as he avoids being hit by a car, a bicycle, and another car, the sounds of the horns and the bicycle rider's, "Watch out where you're going," interrupting the mournful strain of the music.

As the depressed Shell passes a lamp post he sees a piece of Johnny's bandage. To emphasize the discovery, the camera first shows Shell's reaction followed by a cut to a close-up of the bandage wrapped around the bottom of the post and blowing in the wind. The camera pans slightly left as we see Shell reach into the frame and take the bandage. The bandage is evidence that Johnny earlier has taken the same route from the junk yard to the saloon. Shell continues to handle the bandage, first smelling it to detect the presence of blood, and then bunching it in his hands behind him as he furtively enters the saloon.

The camera records Shell's thought processes as he tries to piece together clues that will lead him to Johnny. Shell's purposeful movements, which contrast with the relaxed milling about of the patrons in the saloon, are watched by Fencie. Shell suddenly stops and there is a cut to a close-up of the crib door showing the paper which had earlier been wedged as an improvised latch. (A sequence of shots associated more with Shell than any other character in the film is the shot of him reacting followed by a close-up of what he is reacting to.) Shell has found the final clue and starts to walk slowly toward the crib. Fencie stops Shell's progress with an offer of a drink. While outwardly trying to respond to Fencie pleasantly, Shell's displeasure is subtly caught by the camera.

The tension in the Shell-Fencie sequence is expressed by close-ups of the two and their subdued conversation in contrast to the activity around them. Shell repeats his double entendre conversation about his "bird" and its "hurted wing." The transition from Fencie's patronizing tone about this trivial matter to his realization that the bird is Johnny is skillfully realized by the acting of William Hartnell supported by Krasker's camera. As Shell and Fencie talk guardedly about Johnny, the frequency of close shots increases. Fencie tries to bluff and dismiss Shell, who, in turn, moves closer to him.

At this moment, the sudden entrance of Lukey, expected but forgotten, pushes the scene in a different direction. Lukey enters and characteristically bullies a man out of his path. Shell's action has changed from attempting to get Johnny from Fencie into avoiding Lukey. Lukey continues to think about Johnny's eyes as he talks to a man at the bar. Lukey's desire to paint Johnny and put on the canvas the truth of life and death is negated by his past failures which hang above the bar.

While Lukey speaks, the man at the bar blows smoke past his face. One is reminded of the sequence when Lukey, sitting in front of the stove, discussed the faces in the fire with Tober. The association is important because, as Lukey dismisses his tavern murals as work done for "beer money," there is a cut to Johnny slumped over a table. Johnny knocks over a beer glass and thus begins a sequence in which the film returns to the expressionistic style of the earlier scenes dramatizing Johnny's delirium by the subjective camera. A large close-up of Johnny is followed by a close-up of the spilled beer. Alwyn's music introduced at this point is similar to that used during the sequence when Johnny hallucinated the girl on the skate as a prison guard. The sudden change from the objective to the subjective camera has been prepared. In addition, Lukey watching the faces in the fire has forshadowed Johnny seeing in the beer bubbles the faces of the people he has encountered during his odyssey.

The camera quickly moves close to the bubbles on the table as the face of the clerk is seen pointing a gun at Johnny. Faces dissolve into other faces as in succession Johnny sees Rosie and Maudie, Gin Jimmy, and Harry in the bubble. Interspersed are cuts to Johnny's face which grows more pained as the images flash in front of him. Finally, the bubbles are filled with faces all speaking at once, some accusing, some mocking, some comforting. In one brief sequence are reminders of all that has gone before, all that Johnny has experienced, pulled together in the striking image of the faces in the beer bubbles all speaking to Johnny who tries but cannot understand the onslaught of words.

Johnny raises his head and leans back in what appears to be, but is not, slow motion as the sequence builds dramatically to his scream. In a striking series of shots, the camera shows Johnny about to scream and cuts to a high shot looking down over the patrons who react to Johnny's scream heard off camera. This shot is followed by a close-up from a low camera of Lukey and the patrons at the bar. Johnny's scream is sustained as Shell is shown in close-up lowering his glass of beer. The scene seemingly has been built to promise that Johnny will be discovered. However, in a brilliant directorial stroke, Reed suddenly diverts attention from Johnny for a second time, throwing the focus on Lukey and Shell. Lukey sees Shell and breaks the silence with his line, "There's that little rat!"

What follows is mayhem as Lukey tries to catch Shell and in the process nearly destroys the saloon.

The sequence has its humorous moments, an example of the integration of serious and comic elements, as Shell spins several of the barmen around while scrambling behind the bar. Later in the melee, the barmen inadvertently put Lukey and Shell in the same crib causing further havoc. Shell manages a kick into Lukey's midsection before running from the saloon. The barman puts the clock to five minutes past ten, attempting to empty the saloon by indicating that it is past closing time; he is rewarded by a drink thrown in his face. The act is comic, but also evocative if the viewer recalls how Johnny's life is measured by the passing of time on clock faces throughout the film.

Fencie tells Lukey that the damage is "twenty-five quid." (The Lukey of the film is not so extreme as the character portrayed in the novel: damage to the saloon in that version is two hundred and twenty pounds.) Fencie proposes that Lukey take Johnny away in repayment for the damage and as an alternative to prison. Ironically, Johnny is precisely what Lukey wants. Johnny is shown by the camera as no more than a rag doll when first we see his head cradled in Fencie's arm and then see him slump against Lukey. Johnny's fate is placed between Fencie, who is anxious to get rid of him, and Lukey, who wants to paint him, but for the moment is more interested in a drink.

As the pair are driven away in a cab, the tension of the sequence is released momentarily by another comic moment. One of the barmen has been left inside the cab by mistake; he stops the car and tells all who are responsible, "Have you no manners?" The cab moves off again down the snowy street and there is a cut to Lukey telling Johnny that he has a friend who will fix his arm. As if to answer who the "friend" is, the scene dissolves to Lukey's studio where Tober, still wearing his hat and overcoat, is shown sprawled in an overstuffed chair eating fish and chips. One's first reaction is concern that Johnny's life is about to be placed in the hands of this man. However, the scene that follows reveals Tober not only as a healer of the body, but also a character who expands the philosophic thrust of the film.

The images in the scene becomes more fantastic as the story

moves deeper into allegory. Tober is first seen lying in the chair next to the smoking stove. In the background, Shell's head appears through a missing section of the door. There is a close-up of Shell with his mouth open holding a tooth as he asks Tober for help. Shell's concern for his tooth establishes Tober's medical training which shortly will be put to use in caring for Johnny's more serious wound. Shell moves rapidly from pain to hunger as he watches Tober eat.

The entrance of Lukey carrying Johnny over his shoulder is recorded by an extreme low shot. Tober, who has previously been lethargic as well as enigmatic, suddenly moves quickly to help Johnny. The chimes are ringing as Johnny is placed in the chair. The dominant image of the scene is Lukey painting Johnny while Tober, now in his shirt sleeves, tries to clean and bandage his wounds. To intensify the image, Lukey has directed a light on Johnny and placed a palette behind his neck to keep his lifeless face erect. If taken on a realistic level, the scene is macabre, but images and dialogue have combined to push *Odd Man Out* further and further beyond realism.

The dialogue in the scene at Lukey's studio is as allegorical as any in the film. One could argue that the dialogue is too obvious, that too much is baldly stated rather than revealed through action. Some of the dialogue seems unnecessarily packed with "significance." At times, Reed does give the characters business which helps to undercut the explicit philosophy. For example, Shell, wincing from his painful tooth, devours his fish and chips while discussing "faith" with Tober. Shell feels that in losing Johnny he has lost his opportunity for the "particle of faith" hinted at by Father Tom. Tober's responses to Shell's questions are abstruse. When Shell asks, "What does it mean—Faith?" Tober answers, "Only one man had it." Shell repeats the question, "What is it, Tober?" Tober answers, "It's life." At this point Lukey bursts through the door carrying Johnny. With his many synoptic comments about life and death, Tober emerges as the superior thinker in the film, and, at the same time, the most abstract of the principal characters.

One of the problems with the scene is that seemingly more questions are raised than answered. What relates the scene and the philosophy expressed in it to the rest of the film is the brooding sense of fatalism made explicit in the dialogue. Lukey tells Tober that Johnny's life is lost already: "—Patching up his body just so that he can be tried and executed." Tober, who says that this is not his concern, applies the sense of fatalism to not only Johnny but to everyone. He enlarges the story from Johnny's suffering and fate to the suffering and fate of all mankind. When Lukey says, "There's something to be said about him before he dies"; Tober responds, "And about all of us." Later Tober warns Lukey, who thinks he sees something in Johnny's eyes, to take care that he does not find something that he does not understand, that will frighten him. The sequence of lines that follow almost as a litany contains the thematic kernel of the film:

LUKEY: It's the truth about us all.
TOBER: Is that all.
LUKEY: He's doomed.
TOBER: So are we all.
SHELL: Is he really dyin', Tober?
TOBER: We're all dyin'.

Related to the theme of fatalistic suffering is the theme of charity which is extended when the film returns to Lukey's studio.

Alternate scenes at Father Tom's and on the docks interrupt the scene at Lukey's studio. The dialogue between Father Tom and the constable continues the movement of the film into the abstraction of a morality play. Rather than being conflicting characters, Father Tom and the constable seem to represent a debate between mercy and justice. In response to Father Tom's question, "From your experiences with men and women, would you say they're all bad?", the constable answers, "In my position, there's neither good nor bad. There's innocence and guilt, that's all." Later in the sequence when the constable asks Father Tom where Johnny is, Father Tom answers, "Out there somewhere. Amidst the storms of the city." The fact that the camera shows Father Tom looking out at the stormy night gives his words a broader application than a specific reference to Johnny.

The chimes sound more frequently as *Odd Man Out* moves toward its inevitable conclusion. Numerous shots of Kathleen show her reaction to the chiming away of time as she desperately tries to find Johnny. When the constable drives up to Father Tom's, the fog horn sounds to remind Kathleen that the boat, the last means of escape, will be leaving without Johnny. In a brief scene on the docks, Kathleen persuades the seaman to give her more time. Midnight is established as the latest possible time he can wait. After that his ship would be grounded. The chimes are sounding as the scene dissolves back to Lukey's studio with its familiar tableau of Johnny seated in the chair, Tober bandaging him, and Lukey painting.

The chimes continue while Lukey and Tober remain silently engrossed in their respective tasks, Lukey trying to capture the essence of Johnny's soul on canvas and Tober trying to save Johnny's body. The first words are spoken by Shell who is shown in close-up intently watching Tober work. As Shell tells Tober he could have been a great doctor, one becomes aware of a painting of Shell in the background. Unlike the earlier saintly pose, this painting is a mirror of the subject to the very hat, scarf, and coat that he is wearing. The image is important for Johnny's fantasizing the movement of the paintings. As the scene develops, Tober somewhat revives Johnny and wants to send him to the hospital. Lukey insists that Johnny should remain until he finishes painting him. Shell joins the argument to claim his right to take Johnny to Father Tom's in order to claim the promised "particle of faith." As the dispute rages, the camera moves close to Johnny and music is introduced.

In the sequence that follows, Krasker's camera again eloquently captures Johnny's vision during his suffering and delirium. His condition is first indicated by rocking the camera. There is a cut from a pained, wide-eyed expression on his face to a full shot of the studio where the paintings of grotesque caricatures float down the walls and form rows in the room. Sound is also subjective as the voices of Tober and Lukey arguing off camera grow increasingly distant and indistinct. Johnny's hallucinations are momentarily interrupted when Shell asks him about Father Tom. The mention of Father Tom starts Johnny thinking of the priest and his teachings. The images become more haunting as Johnny now sees Father Tom superimposed on the paintings. Johnny, speaking for the first time since the scene at Fencie's saloon, leans forward to address Father Tom, "Tell me, Father—like you used to tell us." In an effective series of shots, Johnny strains to hear the words of Father Tom who stands superimposed on the paintings smiling and gesturing while the argument between Lukey and Tober echoes loudly. Johnny, who has been urging Father Tom to speak louder, verbalizes the visual metaphor: "We've always drowned your voice with our shouting, haven't we, Father? We never really listened to you. We've repeated the words without thinking what they meant."

The words are significant because Father Tom, although an ineffectual and conventional priest, has been portrayed as the morality figure of mercy, a quality lacking in many of the characters in the film. The sense of the speech is applicable not only to Johnny but to mankind. Johnny's following lines represent a return to his childhood, the period when Father Tom taught him: "I remember—when I was a boy—I spoke as a child . . . I thought as a child . . . I understood as a child. But when I became a man I put away childish things." In a strongly dramatic moment, the camera tilts to an extreme low angle as Johnny rises and recites the passage from St. Paul. The contrast between the innocence of childhood and the cynicism of manhood is double edged. Johnny sees childhood as a time when mercy and charity were understood. (Against that view, the children depicted in *Odd Man Out,* with few exceptions, are neither innocent nor merciful.) A possible interpretation of the sequence is that Johnny, who has been unable to hear Father Tom, now gives one of Father Tom's sermons remembered from his childhood.

As Johnny rises to leave the studio he lunges forward pulling the light cord which brings down Lukey's easel and painting, thwarting his effort to capture the truth in Johnny's eyes. Lukey's disgust and despair give a dramatic conclusion to the scene. The focus is now on the final stages of Johnny's wanderings.

All the production elements combine effectively to push the climax of *Odd Man Out* to almost operatic proportions. In a realistic film, the ending might seem overdone. But the movement of *Odd Man Out* has been away from realism and the final effects are appropriate to the style of the film. Alwyn's music brilliantly supports the high emotions achieved.

An image not easily forgotten is Johnny staggering through the snow while Shell urges and encourages him to keep walking. James Mason communicates Johnny's suffering with artful restraint. McCormick plays Shell masterfully in the sequence, walking the thin line between comedy and tragedy with the ease of a high wire artist. His improvised conversation in the doorway as he tries to keep Johnny from being recognized by two men, his waving to the police as they shine a light on him, his concern about having snow in his shoe are examples of fine acting by this unheralded artist.

The direction of the scene is crisp and the action moves quickly from sequence to sequence. Reed makes a final use of the child motif. After Shell pushes Johnny behind a shrub to keep the police from seeing him, Reed follows a shot of Johnny lying in the snow with a close shot of two boys looking out the window at the falling snow. The sequence is repeated with Johnny shown trying to raise himself up from the snow followed by a cut to the boys looking out and finally closing the drape. The contrast is telling: the snow only adds to Johnny's suffering, but to the boys inside their house the falling snow is something to enjoy, something to ride a sled or to-boggan on.

Once Kathleen has found Johnny the pitch of film rises still higher. Reed builds strongly to the encounter between Johnny and Kathleen by using very short sequences and dissolves. As Shell complains that his shoe is full of snow and ice, Kathleen is shown exiting from the frame leaving Shell hopping on one leg. Shell breaking his shoelace is another symbol of impending death, as earlier in the film, Johnny broke his shoelace before the robbery. There is a dissolve to a close pan shot of Johnny staggering weakly along the path, his shadow large on the store fronts, which also re-flect the pointed tops of the iron railings. There is another dissolve to Kathleen running forward under the archways and exiting past the camera. A quick dissolve to Johnny catches him moving under the arches. We are made to feel more of Johnny's suffering as we see him fall backward against the fence. The next sequence of shots shows Johnny in a Christ-like pose agonizing against his cross, the iron fence. There is a close-up of Johnny breathing heavily, fol-lowed by a shot down the passage of Johnny raising his right hand high as he struggles for support against the railings. As Johnny pulls himself along the railings, there is a cut to Kathleen running across the square, the clock tower looming large behind her.

A series of alternating close shots of Johnny and Kathleen show the meeting of the ill-fated pair, supported by Alwyn's imposing music. Kathleen urges Johnny to come to her. He tries but cannot, ("I can't. If you are real stretch out your hand to me"). A medium close shot shows Johnny holding out his hand as Kathleen throws her arms around him. The tableau is held and recorded by a low angle shot which also shows the ominous pointed tops of the iron railing over Johnny's head. Johnny tells Kathleen, "Go back to life, please." But her decision was foreshadowed earlier, to go with him to death.

A blast of the ship's whistle breaks the tableau. Kathleen raises her head from Johnny's shoulder and says, "That's our chance. Will you go with me?" She starts to lead Johnny across the dock square as the scene cuts to Shell and Father Tom on a street corner. The death image is reinforced as Shell continues to fret about his broken lace while Father Tom asks him where Kathleen has gone. The scene cuts back to a long shot of Kathleen leading Johnny across the square.

As the ship moves out to sea, Kathleen sees, but Johnny does not, a police cordon moving forward. A close shot of Kathleen and Johnny in front of the fence is followed by another shot of the cordon with flashlights and headlights playing on the snow, appearing like some impersonal force. For the series of shots leading up to the death of Johnny and Kathleen, Reed moves the camera as near to the characters as at any time during the film. The closeness of the shots is supported by the sound of Johnny's breathing, recorded extremely close to the microphone. There is a close-up as Kathleen puts her arms about Johnny in a love-death embrace. We now see Johnny and Kathleen in a very large close-up. The camera pans over and tilts down as it follows Kathleen's arm down the lapel of Johnny's coat. Another tight close-up follows, showing Kathleen's hand moving into her pocket and taking out a gun.

Reed again edits away from the violent act. Kathleen fires the gun twice and we hear the police return the fire as we see Shell running forward followed by Father Tom. In the novel, Kathleen shoots Johnny and then herself as the police come closer. In the film the guilt is shared as the lines that follow indicate that the police were only firing back in defense.

The bodies of Kathleen and Johnny are shown lying under dark rain coats. We do not see their faces as the camera moves down over the bodies and Father Tom pulls back the covering. The focus is thrown on Father Tom's reaction as he kneels beside them. The long blast of the ship's whistle, the last means of escape, and the tolling of the clock combine with Alwyn's music to underscore the pathos of the scene. Father Tom is shown putting his hand on Shell's shoulder as the two walk off sadly down the street. In the final shot, the camera tilts up to the clock, whose presence has dominated the last part of the film. "The End" appears superimposed as the chimes are sounding midnight.

summary critique

The importance of *Odd Man Out* was recognized in the first wave of reviews which followed the premiere of the film in London and New York. Arthur Vesselo agreed with a number of English critics when he wrote in *Sight and Sound:* "*Odd Man Out* is a sign that our native cinema is reaching maturity. Not the only sign, it is yet among the most complete and certain signs to date, and it is weighty with promise for the future."[28] Peter Noble echoed Vesselo's high praise, calling *Odd Man Out* one of the greatest British films ever made, "a moving, living, breathing work of art." Noble added that *Odd Man Out* would surely be quoted for many years as representative of the highest pinnacle of British postwar production.[29]

Some critics found fault with *Odd Man Out;* their comments related especially to the allegorical approach. However, a recurring statement in a large number of the reviews was that the flaws in *Odd Man Out* could be excused because the film achieved so many ambitious aims. William Whitebait, reflecting this thinking, described *Odd Man Out* as "quite easily the most imaginative film yet produced in England." Whitebait noted some faults in the film— "here and there the dialogue goes on a few seconds longer than it should and the harking after souls produces some awkward moments"—but he felt that they could be forgiven because of the generosity of the vision.[30]

The most perceptive comments on the virtues and flaws of *Odd Man Out* were written, not surprisingly, by James Agee, who was a contributor to both *Time* and *The Nation* when the film premiered in New York. Because Agee's review was published in *The Nation* nearly four months after his review in *Time,* his immediate reactions to the film can be compared to his considered judgments. Some of his findings remain similar, some are enriched, and some become curiously different. Interestingly, Agee's thoughts concerning *Odd Man Out* seem a paradoxical combining of praise and blame in the same judgments. For example, in his *Time* review Agee said that the beauty of the film is at times "so profuse and lovingly planned that it weighs the film down as over-descriptive prose harms a novel."[31] Agee then wrote in *The Nation,* "detail by detail most of *Odd Man Out* is made with great skill and imaginativeness and with a depth of ardor that is very rare in contemporary films."[32] His concluding statement in the *Time* review sums up his respect for *Odd Man Out* despite what he recognized as its problems: "But even in its failures, *Odd Man Out* is admirable. It is a reckless, head-on attempt at greatness, and the attempt frequently succeeds."

Agee was one of the first critics to treat the film as allegory, seeing Johnny McQueen, "at large in the smashing city like a loose bolt in a machine," as representative of Man, anguished and abandoned. Although Agee found *Odd Man Out* an "extraordinary ambitious movie," he felt that the story, after a stunning start, overextended itself and gradually lost contact with humanity. In both reviews, he criticized the increasing use of allegory in the second part of the film. He wrote in *Time:* "Dostoevskian in conception and design, the story progressively becomes more wildly adventurous, more mythical, more half-baked." His review in *The Nation* is more severe on this point: "In the later reels the film, like the novel, tries for a broader and broader allegory and phantasmagoria, but much as I respect this boldness I don't think it succeeds. The story seems merely to ramify too much, to go on too long, and at its unluckiest to go arty." There is no question that *Odd Man Out* does change levels once Johnny leaves the bomb shelter and starts his wanderings through Belfast. Whether the division is a weakness or a strength of the film has been a subject of controversy. Philip T. Hartung, disagreeing with Agee, felt that although cinematically the last half of the film moved more slowly than the first part, it was the thoughtful second half that gave *Odd Man Out* its meaning and extraordinary dignity.[33] Vesselo also saw the film's diverse elements functioning differently: "In it the dramatic intensity which we associate with Hitchcock has been given solidity and meaning by something more than a touch of the tragic poetry which we associate with the Irish playwrights."[34] As Vesselo observed, one of the unique qualities of *Odd Man Out* is putting a religious-philosophic allegory on the thriller structure. Vesselo's allusion to tragic poetry is certainly echoed by Agee, who wrote in his *Time* review that *Odd Man Out* was a rare attempt to use the screen for poetic tragedy.[35]

The most severe critics of *Odd Man Out* objected to what seemed to them a lack of optimism in the film. William Robertson, while admiring the technical accomplishments, asked whether it was all worthwhile to tell such a negative story: "All that brilliant talent spent spent on a film that had hardly any warmth, vitality or love of living at all."[36] He described the film as "beautifully done" but merely horror heaped on pity and pity piled on pathos, the negation of life. Robertson's points, some of which were expressed by other critics as well, were not a mere hankering after a happy ending. Viewed as a totally realistic film and interpreted literally without consideration of the allegorical elements, many episodes in *Odd Man Out* would appear both heartless and negative. Seen as allegory, the same episodes become both distanced and elevated in meaning.

Another point that some critics overlooked was that *Odd Man Out,* while fatalistic, has much vitality. The film shares this quality with the tragedies of the Irish playwrights alluded to by Vesselo. Sean O'Casey called his *Juno and the Paycock* and *The Plough and the Stars* tragedies, but his characters like Joxer Daly, Captain Boyle, Peter Flynn, and Bessie Burgess exist with all their exuberance and frailty in the midst of the tragic events. There is much similar combining of the serious and the comic in the plays of O'Casey and the film of *Odd Man Out*. Characters like Shell, Lukey, or Teresa would not be out of place in an O'Casey play.

Events of the 1970s have moved the Dublin of O'Casey even closer to the Belfast of *Odd Man Out*. In fact, one's understanding of *Odd Man Out* and the character of Johnny could be influenced by the daily reports of the horrors occurring in and around Belfast. Reed's intent in *Odd Man Out* was to use the political unrest in Belfast (described in the screenplay only as "a city in Northern Ireland") as a background to the story of Johnny and his wanderings. Reed carefully kept the focus off the "Organization" and on Johnny's suffering.

Whether or not it is possible to view *Odd Man Out* without reference to contemporary events is difficult to assess. F. L. Green's novel was thought relevant enough to reissue in paperback in 1971 (with a still of James Mason as Johnny on the cover). I feel that the film *Odd Man Out* has been so carefully constructed that the original values of the material would not change significantly if peace had descended in Northern Ireland.

Although many of Reed's films, especially the ones portraying the outcast, use political intrigue as plot material, he has treated the material apolitically. A number of the reviews of *Odd Man Out* and *The Third Man,* for example, took Reed to task for not having a "message" or a "point of view." In a 1947 interview Reed expressed his feelings on the matter: "As a director, I believe my own ideas are not particularly important. What counts is the story value and characterization. Certain people want to put their own ideas about life and politics on film, but I believe that a director has no right to inflict his amateur politics and opinions on an audience."[37]

Discussing his first important film, *The Stars Look Down,* a story that argued for nationalization of the coal mines, Reed observed that the plea for nationalization was implicit in the events and characters. He added that he could have made a picture arguing the reverse of nationalization if the story were valid enough. The question is whether Reed's political or social films lack ethical force because of his refusal to take sides, or whether the films gain added power because he is distanced from the material? Is Harry Lime a more interesting character because Reed does not condemn him for his practices, however odious they might have been? Is Johnny McQueen's odyssey through the streets of Belfast more or less meaningful because Reed is not concerned with the cause for which he gives his life?

Reed's concerns in *Odd Man Out* can be seen by comparing the novel, the advance screenplay, and the finished version of the film. Green's novel is much closer to the tragic violence in present-day Belfast than is the film. The film's violence has been softened during its adaptation from the novel and what violence does occur has been directed by Reed to focus on the implications of the act and not the act itself.

The novel has a series of fights with a high loss of life for both the Organization and the police. The reader is left with the impression of continuous battles between the police and members of the

Organization trying to rescue Johnny. Additional members of the Organization are introduced in the novel, including the character of Seamus who, as second to Johnny, assumes the importance that Dennis has in the film. Seamus, whose philosophy is "act, shoot, and don't be stopping to be nervous," is a rash and trigger happy contrast to Johnny. He is involved in much of the action given to Dennis in the film, including the fight on the tram car. Dennis is drawn quite differently in the novel, where he is so intensely jealous of Johnny that he is killed for no reason during a suicidal attempt at glory. An interesting aspect of the film adaptation is the elimination of Seamus and the strengthening of Dennis.

There are many specific examples of violence in the novel which have been altered in the film. We have noted how the final scene of *Odd Man Out*—the death of Johnny and Kathleen—has been changed to soften the impact. In the novel, Kathleen shoots Johnny and then herself. In the film, she shoots at the police as they advance forcing them to fire back, thus becoming in the adaptation only indirectly responsible for the death of Johnny and herself. Given the elimination and underplaying of much of the violence in the film, Kathleen's pulling the trigger might have been too strong a note on which to end.

Reed, who had much control over the shaping of the screenplay, also softened the violence from draft to draft. For example, Johnny fights two men on the mill steps in both the novel and the advance screenplay, but only one man in the film. Dennis' fight on the tram is much more elaborate in the advance screenplay, with guns firing and Dennis finally beaten to a bloodied pulp by the police. The struggle as it appears in the film is much less violently stated. In the advance screenplay as in the novel, the head constable tilts Kathleen's chin back with the barrel of his revolver while questioning her. In the film, he uses a cane instead, a slight variation that could change the action from threatening to merely authoritarian. Many such changes were made in the evolution of *Odd Man Out* from novel to film. Although some critics pointed to such variations as examples of Reed's political aloofness, perhaps the reason was that the changes more suited Reed's style of direction and, most important, his intent to focus on the allegorical and not the political nature of the story.

When *Odd Man Out* was first presented, the film not only received critical praise but also seemed to appeal to a wide range of audiences in England, the United States, and elsewhere in the world. *Sight and Sound* reported in 1948 that it had become one of the most successful films ever shown in South America. Reed was honored at the Brussels Film Festival and the Venice Film Festival for his direction of the picture. A number of critics, including Hartung, picked *Odd Man Out* as one of the best films of the year. The British Film Yearbook named it the best British film released in 1947, and James Mason was selected by the *Daily Express* as the best actor of 1947 for his performance.

The film has gained in reputation and is often cited by film critics and historians. Roger Manvell wrote in 1969, "Of the hundreds of films made following the war it is impossible to list more than a few to represent the best. Such a list must include Carol Reed's *Odd Man Out, The Fallen Idol,* and *The Third Man.*"[38] A number of books on film have drawn examples of superior techniques from *Odd Man Out,* including *A Seat at the Cinema, The Technique of Film Music,* and *The Technique of Film Editing. Odd Man Out* may have received its most enduring recognition when Harold Pinter used the film prominently in his most recent full length play, *Old Times,* which premiered in 1971. Pinter refers to *Odd Man Out* and three of its actors—Robert Newton, F. J. McCormick, and James Mason—a number of times in speeches between Deeley and Anna, who describe their first meeting during a showing of the film. The use of the film as such an important metaphor in this provocative play, illustrates Pinter's awareness and possibly his respect for it. Pinter's stature as a writer of memorable screenplays along with his works for the theatre gives added significance to his use of *Odd Man Out* in *Old Times.*

Reed's major films have been said to exemplify the best qualities of the British cinema—unparalleled craftsmanship, polished scenarios, and immaculate acting.[39] When Reed made *Odd Man Out,* he was reaching his zenith as a director. The films that preceded *Odd Man Out,* such as *The Way Ahead,* and the films that followed, such as *The Fallen Idol* and *The Third Man,* show Reed at the peak of his powers. What makes *Odd Man Out* a film classic is that Reed the craftsman enabled Reed the artist to shape a film that both deals with and transcends its political-thriller structure. Reed uses allegory successfully to probe the ethical question of charity in man without losing the momentum of story and the richness of characterization. What is remarkable about *Odd Man Out* is the effective telling of a story which could be abstract and grey—a sermon—and making it suspenseful, haunting, comic, vital, and always interesting without losing the profundity for which Reed was striving. Even when the philosophy is slightly confused, the story and the characters are compelling. Even when the *cinema noir* style seems to match the darkness of the human vision, there is a warmth and compassion that somehow manages to be expressed. *Odd Man Out* is a film, both lyric and provocative, which is not easily forgotten.

a Carol Reed filmography
selected bibliography
rental sources
notes

a Carol Reed filmography

1935 *It Happened in Paris* (Codirected by Robert Wyler), with John Loder, Nancy Burne; screenplay by John Huston and H. F. Maltby from the play *L'Arpete* by Yves Mirande.

1935 *Midshipman Easy,* with Margaret Lockwood (in US, *Men of the Seas*), screenplay by Anthony Kimmins.

1936 *Laburnum Grove,* with Edmund Gwenn, Cedric Hardwicke; screenplay by Gordon Wellesley and Anthony Kimmins from the play by J. B. Priestley.

1936 *Talk of the Devil,* with Ricardo Cortez, Sally Eilers; screenplay by Carol Reed, George Barraud, Anthony Kimmins.

1937 *Who's Your Lady Friend?* with Margaret Lockwood, Sarah Churchill; screenplay by Anthony Kimmins and Julius Hoest.

1938 *Bank Holiday,* with Margaret Lockwood, John Lodge (in US, *Three on a Weekend*), screenplay by Rodney Ackland and Roger Burford.

1938 *Penny Paradise,* with Edmund Gwenn, Betty Driver; screenplay by Thomas Thompson and W. L. Meade.

1939 *Climbing High,* with Michael Redgrave, Jessie Mathews, Alistair Sim; screenplay by Stephen Clarkson.

1939 *A Girl Must Live,* with Margaret Lockwood, Lilli Palmer; screenplay by Frank Launder and Austin Melford.

1939 *The Stars Look Down,* with Margaret Lockwood, Michael Redgrave, Emlyn Williams; screenplay by J. B. Williams and A. J. Cronin from the novel by A. J. Cronin.

1940 *Night Train to Munich,* with Rex Harrison, Margaret Lockwood; screenplay by Frank Launder and Sidney Gilliat from the novel by Gordon Wellesley.

1940 *The Girl in the News,* with Margaret Lockwood, Emlyn Williams; screenplay by Frank Launder and Sidney Gilliat from the novel by Roy Vickers.

1941 *Kipps,* with Michael Redgrave, Max Adrian, Phyllis Calvert (in US, *The Remarkable Mr. Kipps*), screenplay by Frank Launder and Sidney Gilliat from the novel by H. G. Wells.

1941 *A Letter from Home,* documentary short subject.

1942 *The Young Mr. Pitt,* with Robert Donat, Phyllis Calvert (made in 1941 and not released until 1942), screenplay by Frank Launder and Sidney Gilliat.

1943 *The New Lot,* documentary.

1944 *The Way Ahead,* expanded version of *The New Lot* with David Niven, Stanley Holloway, William Hartnell, Leo Genn; screenplay by Eric Ambler and Peter Ustinov.

1945 *The True Glory,* documentary (Codirected by Garson Kanin).

1947 *Odd Man Out,* with James Mason, F. J. McCormick, Robert Newton; screenplay by F. L. Green and R. C. Sherriff from the novel by F. L. Green.

1948 *The Fallen Idol,* with Ralph Richardson, Bobby Henrey, Michelle Morgan; screenplay by Graham Greene, Lesley Storm, William Templeton from the story *The Basement Room* by Graham Greene.

1949 *The Third Man,* with Orson Welles, Joseph Cotten, Trevor Howard; screenplay by Graham Greene.

1951 *Outcast of the Islands,* with Trevor Howard, Ralph Richardson; screenplay by William Fairchild from the novel by Joseph Conrad.

1953 *The Man Between,* with James Mason, Claire Bloom; screenplay by Harry Kurnitz and Eric Linklater from the novel *Susanne in Berlin* by Walter Ebert.

1955 *A Kid for Two Farthings,* with Diana Dors, David Kossoff; screenplay by Wolf Mankowitz from his novel.

1956 *Trapeze,* with Burt Lancaster, Gina Lollobrigida, Tony Curtis; screenplay by James R. Webb.

1958 *The Key,* with William Holden, Sophia Loren, Trevor Howard; screenplay by Carl Foreman from the novel *Stella* by Jan de Hartog.

1960 *Our Man in Havana,* with Alec Guinness, Noel Coward, Maureen O'Hara; screenplay by Graham Greene from his novel.

1962 *Mutiny on the Bounty,* with Marlon Brando, Trevor Howard, Richard Harris (Reed replaced as director by Lewis Milestone and given credit as codirector); screenplay by Charles Lederer from the novel by Charles Nordhoff and James Norman Hall.

1963 *The Running Man,* with Laurence Harvey, Lee Remick, Alan Bates; screenplay by John Mortimer from the novel *The Ballad of the Running Man* by Shelley Smith.

1965 *The Agony and The Ecstasy,* with Charlton Heston, Diane Cilento; screenplay by Philip Dunne from the novel by Irving Stone.
1968 *Oliver!* with Oliver Reed, Ron Moody, Mark Lester; screenplay by Vernon Harris, based on the book, music, lyrics by Lionel Bart, adapted from Charles Dickens' *Oliver Twist.*
1971 *Flap,* with Anthony Quinn, Shelley Winters, Victor Jory; screenplay by Clair Huffaker from his novel *Nobody Loves a Drunken Indian.*
1972 *The Public Eye,* with Mia Farrow, Topol, Michael Jayston; screenplay by Peter Shaffer from his short play.

selected bibliography

Agee, James. Review of *Odd Man Out. Time* (March 3, 1947), 81. An excellent review of the film. Agee has high praise for cameraman Robert Krasker. Agee points out the flaws in *Odd Man Out,* but adds, "It is a reckless, head-on attempt at greatness, and the attempt frequently succeeds."
————. Review of *Odd Man Out. Nation* (July 19, 1947), 79–81. Agee praises the depiction of a city at night in the film.
Anonymous. "Sightseeing Tour: Carol Reed, British Director, Checks on the Tastes of American Audiences." *New York Times* (April 6, 1947). Relates Reed's preparations for the release of *Odd Man Out* in the United States.
————. "British Feature Directors: An Index to Their Work." *Sight and Sound* (Autumn 1958), 289–304. A brief but perceptive critique of Reed's work.
Breit, Harvey. " 'I Give the Public What *I* Like.' " *New York Times Magazine* (Jan. 15, 1950), 18–19. Brief discussions of *Odd Man Out, The Fallen Idol,* and *The Third Man* including good stills from the film.

Brown, John Mason. "The Hunt and the Hunted." *The Saturday Review* (May 24, 1947), 22–25. A detailed review of *Odd Man Out* in which Brown cites the "integrity" of the film.

Crowther, Bosley. Review of *Odd Man Out. New York Times* (April 24, 1947). Crowther criticizes the second half of *Odd Man Out:* "the protagonist is shelved for long spells while the author and, perforce, the director go searching for a philosophy of life."

Fawcett, Marion. "Sir Carol Reed." *Films in Review* 3 (March, 1959), 134–41. A survey of Reed's career from his beginnings to the filming of *Our Man in Havana.* The article is not profound but contains some useful biographical material.

Forman, Denis. *Films, 1945–1950.* London: Longmans, Green, 1951. By the director of the Film Institute. Survey of British films and filmmaking. Details contributions of Carol Reed.

Goodman, Ezra. "Carol Reed." *Theatre Arts* 5 (May, 1947), 57–59. Contains useful insights into Reed's philosophy of directing.

Hadsell, John. "Odd Man Out" in *Classics of the Film,* edited by Arthur Lenning. Madison: Wisconsin Film Society Press, 1965 An analysis of *Odd Man Out* which points up Reed's use of "Christian symbolism."

Hartung, Philip T. Review of *Odd Man Out. The Commonweal* 4 (May 9, 1947), 94. Hartung is one of the few contemporary critics who thought the second half of the film superior to the first.

Huntley, John. "Film Music in Britain, 1947–48" in *British Film Yearbook,* edited by Peter Noble. Excellent discussion of William Alwyn's music for *Odd Man Out.*

Huntley, John and Roger Manvell. *The Technique of Film Music.* London: Focal Press, 1957. William Alwyn wrote the introduction to the edition. Contains an analysis of the music scoring for the last scene in *Odd Man Out.* Some good information on Alwyn's philosophy of writing music for the film.

Isaacs, Hermine Rich. "On With the New!" *Theatre Arts* 5 (May, 1947), 49–51. An examination of *Odd Man Out* containing a good discussion of Reed's style of directing.

Kael, Pauline. "The Concealed Art of Carol Reed." *The New Yorker* (December 14, 1968), 193–96. A perceptive review of *Oliver!* which is expanded to examine Reed's craft.

Kennedy, Paul P. "The Carol Reed Formula." *New York Times* (November 30, 1947). A profile of Reed which contains information on Reed's methods of working with actors.

LeJeune, C. A. "Portrait of England's No. 1 Film Director." *New York Times* (September 7, 1941). An informative survey of Reed's early film career to 1941.

Manvell, Roger. *A Seat at the Cinema.* London: Evans Brothers, 1951. Book includes a lengthy review of *Odd Man Out* and a section from the screenplay, the Father Tom–Shell scene. Also includes a scene from *The Way Ahead.*

————. *Three British Screen Plays.* London: Methuen, 1950. Includes the advance screenplay of *Odd Man Out* as originally written—narrative and dialogue are given without the full technical breakdown. Also includes screenplays of *Brief Encounter* and *Scott of the Antarctic.*

McCarten, John. Review of *Odd Man Out. The New Yorker* (May 3, 1947), 71–79. McCarten voices a common critical view that *Odd Man Out's* symbolism weighs down the second half of the film.

O'Hara, Shirley. Review of *Odd Man Out. The New Republic* (May 12, 1947). A perceptive review of the film. Reed "can make a camera give you a sensory reaction. Often without people, photographing streets and buildings and details, he can conjure more than nausea and a dreadful malaise: he projects fear."

Polonsky, Abraham. *"Odd Man Out* and *Monsieur Verdoux." Hollywood Quarterly* 4 (July, 1947): 401–407. Film director Polonsky reviews *Odd Man Out* from the view of the film as "a fantasy of the unconscious."

Reisz, Karel. *The Technique of Film Editing.* New York: Communication Arts Books, 1953. A valuable study of the history and practice of editing which contains an analysis of the robbery sequence from *Odd Man Out.* Reisz is an important British film director.

Rothe, Anna, editor. "Carol Reed," in *Current Biography*. New York: H. W. Wilson Company, 1950. A biographical survey of Reed's career to 1950. Contains some useful information dealing with Reed's apprenticeship as an actor and director in theatre.

Sarris, Andrew. "Carol Reed in the Context of His Time." *Film Culture* 4 (1956), 14–17 and 1 (1957), 11–14. Sarris' two-part article is one of the best studies of Reed's work. Premise of the article is that Reed, "more than any other director, has occupied the middle ground between Italian neo-realism and British formalism."

Symmonds, Julia. "Reflections on 'Odd Man Out.' " *Film Quarterly* (Summer, 1947), 52–56. Symmonds' article, which appeared in the final issue of Peter Noble's short-lived journal, concentrates on the weaknesses of *Odd Man Out*.

Vesselo, Arthur. Review of *Odd Man Out*. *Sight and Sound* 61 (Spring, 1947), 39–40. The importance of *Odd Man Out* to British film is recognized by Vesselo: *"Odd Man Out* is a sign that our native cinema is reaching maturity."

Voigt, Michael. "Pictures of Innocence: Sir Carol Reed." *Focus on Films* (Spring, 1974), 17–38. Survey of Reed's career, also contains stills from films and a good Reed filmography.

Weatherby, W. J. "The Director Who Is Never Satisfied." *The Guardian* (November 27, 1959). In the interview section of the article, Reed makes some interesting comments concerning his relationship with the screen writer.

Whitehall, Richard. "The Stars Look Down." *Films and Filming* 4 (January, 1962). Part of a "great films of the century" series, the article contains a critical summary and a detailed account of the history of the early Reed success.

Wilson, Harry. "Seven Directors," in *British Film Yearbook*, edited by Peter Noble. London: Skelton Robinson, 1949. A brief discussion of Reed's work up to *Odd Man Out*.

Whitebait, William. Review of *Odd Man Out*. *The New Statesman and Nation* (February 8, 1947). Whitebait calls *Odd Man Out*, "quite easily the most imaginative film yet produced in England."

rental and purchase sources

Astral Films Ltd.
224 Davenport Road
Toronto 5, Ontario, Canada

Canfilm Screen Service Ltd.
522–11th Avenue S. W.
Calgary, Alberta, T2R 0C8, Canada

Janus Films, Inc.
745 Fifth Avenue
New York, New York   10022

Janus Films, Inc.
1228 15th Street
Larimer Square
Denver, Colorado   80202

notes

1. Ezra Goodman, "Carol Reed," *Theatre Arts* 31 (May, 1947), 57.
2. Pauline Kael, "The Concealed Art of Carol Reed," *The New Yorker* (December 14, 1968), 196.
3. Denis Forman, *Films, 1945–1950* (London: Longmans, Green, 1951), 15.
4. *New York Times* (December 20, 1940), 21.
5. Harry Wilson, "Seven Directors," *British Film Yearbook,* ed., Peter Noble (London: Skelton Robinson, 1949), 71.

6. *New York Times* (July 24, 1941), 15.
7. Andrew Sarris, "Carol Reed in the Context of His Time," *Film Culture* 2 (1956), 15.
8. James Agee, *Nation* (July 19, 1947), 269.
9. Forman, 15.
10. W. J. Weatherby, "The Director Who Is Never Satisfied," *Guardian* (November 26, 1959), 8.
11. Michael Redgrave, *Mask or Face* (New York: Theatre Arts Books, 1958), 135.
12. C. A. LeJeune, "Portrait of England's No. 1 Film Director," *New York Times* (September 7, 1941), 3.
13. Sarris, "Carol Reed in the Context of His Time," Part 2, *Film Culture* 3 (1957), 14.
14. Graham Greene, "The Third Man as a Story and a Film," *New York Times* (March 19, 1950), 19.
15. Sarris, Part 2, 12.
16. Agee, *Time* (March 3, 1947), 368.
17. Agee, *Nation* (July 19, 1947), 269.
18. Karel Reisz, *The Technique of Film Editing* (New York: Communication Arts Books, Hastings House, 1953), 268.
19. John Huntley, "Film Music in Britain, 1947–48," *British Film Yearbook,* ed., Peter Noble (London: Skelton Robinson, 1948), 39.
20. Huntley and Roger Manvell, *The Technique of Film Music* (London: Focal Press, 1957), 202. In Reed, Alwyn found a director who thought of music while shooting a film. Throughout his career, Reed had tried to evolve a central music idea which emphasized the main theme of the story. An example is the zither music played by Anton Karas for *The Third Man.* Reed wanted the melancholy notes of the zither to evoke a nostalgia for a Vienna trying to recapture its past against the postwar realities of survival. In *The Man Between,* the phrase on the saxaphone evoked the image of a ruined Berlin. Similar characterizing motifs are found in *The Fallen Idol* and *A Kid for Two Farthings.*
21. Ibid.
22. Edward Garrick, comp., *Art and Design in the British Film* (New York: Arno Press, 1972), 61.

23. Reisz, 266.
24. Roger Manvell, *A Seat at the Cinema* (London: Evans Brothers, 1951), 182.
25. Reisz, 267.
26. F. L. Green, *Odd Man Out* (North Hollywood: Leisure Books, 1971), 35.
27. Ibid., 50.
28. Arthur Vesselo, "British Films of the Quarter," *Sight and Sound* 16 (Spring, 1947), 40.
29. Peter Noble, "Films of the Year," *British Film Yearbook,* ed., Peter Noble (London: Skelton Robinson, 1950), 12–13.
30. William Whitebait, *New Statesman and Nation* (February 8, 1947), 113.
31. Agee, *Time* (March 3, 1947), 81.
32. Agee, *Nation* (July 19, 1947), 269.
33. Philip T. Hartung, *Commonweal* (May 9, 1947), 94.
34. Vesselo, 39.
35. Agee, *Time* (March 3, 1947), 81.
36. William Robertson, *Sight and Sound* 21 (Summer, 1948), 92.
37. Goodman, 57.
38. Roger Manvell, *New Cinema in Britain* (London: E. P. Dutton, 1969), 15.
39. Alex Grant, Canadian Film Institute notes for Carol Reed–Don Siegel festival, April 4 to May 16, 1974.